Forms of Performance

From J.S. Bach to M. Alunno (1972-)

Edited by
Michael Maul
Bach-Archiv Leipzig, Germany
Alberto Nones
Associazione Europea di Musica e Comunicazione (AEMC), Italy;
Conservatory of Music of Gallarate, Italy

Series in Music

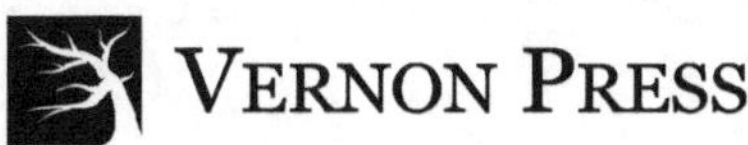

www.vernonpress.com

In the Americas:
Vernon Press
1000 N West Street,
Suite 1200, Wilmington,
Delaware 19801
United States

In the rest of the world:
Vernon Press
C/Sancti Espiritu 17,
Malaga, 29006
Spain

Series in Music

Library of Congress Control Number: 2019949468

ISBN: 978-1-62273-915-8

Also available:

978-1-62273-824-3 [Hardback]; 978-1-62273-857-1 [Hardback, CD Edition];

978-1-62273-865-6 [PDF, E-Book]

The audio tracks for this title can be downloaded here:
https://vernonpress.com/book/883

This publication was issued upon acceptance of the papers by Vernon Press and the AEMC Scientific Committee, formed by Dr. Ricciarda di Belgiojoso, Professor Monika Fink, Dr. Michael Maul, Dr. Alberto Nones and Dr. Hamish Robb, which also oversaw the peer review process.

Table of contents

List of figures

List of Figures

Introduction

by Alberto Nones

Associazione Europea di Musica e Comunicazione (AEMC), Italy; Conservatory of Music of Gallarate, Italy

This volume is the result of the 2nd AEMC Conference on Music, Communication and Performance, organized by the Associazione Europea di Musica e Comunicazione (AEMC) and held in Montecassiano on June 29-30, 2019. The conference comprised papers and performances, a selection of those appearing in this book and in the attached audio CD. The sub-focus of the conference was on Johann Sebastian Bach, and a number of contributions centered on this subject. The topic of music performance, though, was approached from a much broader variety of angles and the present volume gives a fair representation of the breadth and richness of the authors' and performers' perspectives. It is divided into two parts, the first focusing on J. S. Bach research, and the second on other studies. The division is straightforward but not without consequence. Today, Bach represents one of the most revered and studied figures in the history of classical music, despite a time during which he was almost forgotten. And the second part of the book deals with composers who are active today, like Marco Alunno, or with composers from the recent past who are less known and performed, such as Pietro Cimara and Leo Ornstein. The attempt of this book and CD is to encourage fresh approaches to the study of a monument like Bach, while also encouraging original research of modern composition and performance. This book's form is thus based on the belief that the history of music is comprised of many figures, some undeservedly forgotten, and that our understanding of and approach to music is at once both shaped by the past and directed by constantly changing sounds and attitudes of the present.

To begin the section on Bach studies, Michael Maul's paper exemplifies the approach of a Bach scholar who is also a genuine admirer of an unsurpassable master's art. Specifically, Maul argues that Bach's 200 existing sacred cantatas are a playground in which one can discover and enjoy the very heart of J. S. Bach's art—despite many of them not featuring in the shortlist of the most canonical masterworks. Maul contends that, although these works were composed under constant time pressure as occasional works for given

Sundays, churches, and congregations, they can nowadays be considered a timeless repertoire soaring across geographical and religious borders. The paper focuses on several cantatas, comprising pieces from Bach's early Mühlhausen and Weimar periods to his mature Leipzig work, in order to demonstrate the range of innovations in terms of text-music relationships, instrumentation, and the intermingling of musical genres and styles. Chiara Bertoglio's paper analyses the Italian transcriptions for piano two hands of Bach's Sonatas and Partitas for solo violin. The transcendental technical and musical demands of these works, besides the demands they pose on the listeners, often discouraged their public performance. The paper examines the approaches to these works through the lense of the creation, by Italian musicians, of numerous virtuoso piano transcriptions of single movements from the Sonatas and Partitas. They range from Busoni's famous Chaconne, to less known but fascinating transcriptions by Riccardo Pick-Mangiagalli and Sergio Fiorentino. Through this study, Bertoglio also throws light on the historical changes in the style of writing and performing Bach in the past century, contributing to the broader issue of Bach reception in Italy. Maria Borghesi's paper is dedicated to the reception of Johann Sebastian Bach's Sonatas and Partitas as a milestone body of works for both pedagogy and virtuosic performance. Borghesi inquires into the Italian reception of Sonatas and Partitas in the late twentieth century, focusing on two specific sets of oppositions: firstly, how the structure of the Sonatas and Partitas allowed performers and music organizers to conceive of them as either coherent collections, or as a series of distinct pieces which were suitable for showing the performers' technical and musical skills; and secondly, how these works could be, and have been, considered as either the latest violin masterworks of the Baroque era, or as the first witness of modern instrumental technique. Borghesi's aim is to show how diverse premises entailed different reception-phenomena in the complex web constituted by performers, concert life, and the Italian discographic market. Quite diverse is the context discussed in Francisco Castillo's paper, which takes us to the use of Bach in music education in Latin America. The issue of Bach's reception here becomes as fascinating as it is problematic. Music education in Latin America, argues Castillo, faces several challenges, the hardest one being the problem of overcoming a Eurocentric history in which biographies of canonical composers, and the use of their music, have played a critical role. The paper identifies the different uses of J. S. Bach in music education in Latin America, from its consolidation as a representative of the Baroque era to a model of technical complexity, from the view of the founder of both tonal theory and tempered tuning to a symbol of personal improvement and as a father of Western music, or indeed of Music as such. Identifying the ideologies and metaphors that openly or indirectly operate in such an influential story,

Castillo is able to underline how Bach's shadow has influenced how people think of music in Latin America. Castillo contends that the emphasis on Bach, and on myths surrounding Bach, has made other important elements of the musical phenomenon invisible in certain circles. Among these other elements are the musical practices, routes of circulation, orality, and dance.

Interestingly enough, musical practice, circulation, orality—in one word, musicking (Small 1998)—were not alien at all to how J. S. Bach may have conceived of and experienced music during his own time, that is, as a real human being, in everyday contexts (Wolff 2001), and separate from the mythographic picture through which many have tried to make sense of his music and figure over the centuries. It is a healthy counterpoint, therefore, to contrast a set of Bach studies with a dive into lesser-known composers of our recent past, as well as into the work of a contemporary composer. To start with, Andrés Ruiz focuses on futurism, an artistic movement that may not be of primary concern for musicians and musicologists but which has played a major role in the development of new art in the twentieth century in several countries, including the United States. Leo Ornstein, for one, was deeply influenced by futurism, especially in some of his early piano music, Ruiz argues. Ornstein's pianism is evidently full of remnants of compositional inheritances, just as it is full of new exploratory challenges and unusual sounds, most notably derived by a combination of mechanism and noise in piano writing. Ruiz's paper, like his performance in the CD, aims to prove that one can identify a link between conservationism and futurism in Ornstein's early piano music, which is a key link, arguably, in any new artistic creation. Alberto Nones's paper, too, has to do in some way with the theme of preserving elements of tradition and adding new elements in the process of artistic creation. Nones examines and compares two art song versions, dating from the early 1930s, of an 1819 famous idyll by Italian poet Giacomo Leopardi, *L'Infinito.* One is by semi-unknown composer Pietro Cimara, and the other by Mario Castelnuovo-Tedesco. Through musical analysis, followed by a performance of the two pieces that can be heard in the CD attached, the comparison aims to show how a different reading of the same poem, on the part of the composers, can result in important and rich musical differences. Nones suggests that Pietro Cimara's musical reading anticipates an interpretation of the poem (and of the poet) which has come to the fore recently, whereas the other reading, by Mario Castelnuovo-Tedesco, conforms to more traditional visions of Leopardi as the exponent of a pessimist view of man and the world. The hypothesis that music can indeed express pessimism, or optimism, or any other human sentiment and vision, lies at the center of Nones's paper, which also attempts to single out some of those music elements that may vehicle such effects on the listener. Alunno's and Gómez Bravo's paper, endowed with the typical hands-on approach of the composer and of the interpreter, testifies how, in the literature for solo instrument, etudes typically present different kinds of technical and expressive challenges. Such works often focus on single problematic aspects of performance on a specific instrument. The piano etudes by Marco Alunno have such an analytical purpose as well, although, in some cases, they recall writing techniques and melodic-rhythmical modules usually associated with composers and styles of both the past, with a reference to J. S. Bach *in primis*, and present times. In particular, three etudes ("Expressive Fingering", "Parallel Thirds" and "Broken Octaves") are briefly described and analyzed from both a compositional and an interpretive approach, and these can be heard in the CD attached.

Indeed, recordings of performances given over the two days of the conference have been included either to clarify arguments made in the papers, or to more generally testify to the music explored. The technical quality of the recordings has been deemed sufficient for this purpose although it is not of professional standard, especially as regards Ciferri's and Luisi's performances, which were compromised by a buzzing sound (which gives, nevertheless, a certain vintage feeling that may be heard as evoking the distance that separates us from the music being played). Thanks go to Mayor Dr. Leonardo Catena and the municipality of Montecassiano, with special mention of Ilaria Palmieri whose efforts are invaluable, for assistance in organizing the conference.

References

Small, C.N.C. (1998). *Musicking: The Meanings of Performing and Listening*, Hanover, Wesleyan University Press.

Wolff, C. (2000). *Johann Sebastian Bach: The Learned Musician*, London and New York, W.W. Norton.

Part I

Chapter 1

Musical border crossings in J. S. Bach's sacred *Cantatas*

by Michael Maul

Bach-Archiv Leipzig, Germany

The Leipzig "Ring of *Cantatas*"—a unique celebration of Bach's *Cantatas*

In 2019 at the annual Leipzig Bachfest, a remarkably successful concert cycle took place named the "Ring of Cantatas". This cycle goes back to an idea conceived by Sir John Eliot Gardiner and me in 2016 when we both thought it might be a good approach to put the 30 best Bach sacred cantatas into a cycle performed at the Leipzig Bachfest in a very short time frame—in 10 concerts on only one weekend—in Bach's two Leipzig churches—the St. Thomas and the St. Nicholas. It was quite a challenge to organize this cycle. After some discussion, we decided to invite all the conductors and groups to perform in the cycle, who already had recorded all of Bach's sacred cantatas. Besides Gardiner himself with his Monteverdi Choir and the English Baroque Soloists, these were Ton Koopman with his Amsterdam Baroque Orchestra & Choir, Masaaki Suzuki and his Bach Collegium Japan, the Gächinger Cantory under its new conductor Hans-Christoph Rademann (instead of Helmuth Rilling) and—of course—Bach's Leipzig St. Thomas Boys Choir under the direction of Bach's successor Gotthold Schwarz. However, when preparing the cycle, the most challenging part for us was to decide which 30 sacred cantatas actually represent the "Top 30", since there is, of course, no official ranking of all of the 200 existent Bach cantatas, and it would obviously be impossible to create such a ranking based on objective criteria.

So here is the story of how we created our list. We decided to play a game. John Eliot Gardiner, who was in 2016 president of the Bach-Archive Leipzig, Peter Wollny, director of the Bach-Archive, and I, first of all, had to decide independently from one another which were the "30 best" from nearly 200 Bach cantatas—a thanklessly subjective undertaking. An impossible undertaking, in fact, as I found out over the next few days; after many truly heart-rending decisions, when only 33 titles were left on my list, I found myself incapable of striking off any more works. For my fellow "strikers", it was the same: a heavyhearted John Eliot Gardiner presented me with a list of 38 pieces, and Peter Wollny concluded that for him, Bach's "30 best" cantatas actually numbered at least 52.

DIE 30 ›BESTEN‹ KANTATEN / THE 30 ›BEST‹ CANTATAS

ERGEBNIS DER UMFRAGE / RESULTS OF A SURVEY

unter / *among* Sir John Eliot Gardiner (JEG), Michael Maul (MM), Peter Wollny (PW)

I. KANTATEN MIT DE-TEMPORE-BESTIMMUNG / CANTATAS FOR THE CHURCH YEAR

Nun komm, der Heiden Heiland, BWV 61 (1. Advent)	MM
Schwingt freudig euch empor, BWV 36 (1. Advent)	JEG
Wachet! betet! betet! wachet!, BWV 70[a] (2. Advent)	JEG, MM
Christen, ätzet diesen Tag, BWV 63 (1. Weihnachtstag)	JEG
Gelobet seist du, Jesu Christ, BWV 91 (1. Weihnachtstag)	PW
Unser Mund sei voll Lachens, BWV 110 (1. Weihnachtstag)	JEG, PW
Jauchzet, frohlocket, BWV 248/1 (1. Weihnachtstag)	MM
Süßer Trost, mein Jesus kömmt, BWV 151 (3. Weihnachtstag)	JEG, MM, PW
Jesu, nun sei gepreiset, BWV 41 (Neujahr)	MM
Sie werden aus Saba alle kommen, BWV 65 (Epiphanias)	PW
Herr, wie du willt, BWV 73 (3. So. n. Epiph.)	PW
Jesus schläft, was soll ich hoffen, BWV 81 (4. So. n. Epiph.)	JEG
Ich habe genung, BWV 82 (Mariae Reinigung)	JEG, MM, PW
Mit Fried und Freud, BWV 125 (Marae Reinigung)	PW
Erhalt uns, Herr, bei deinem Wort, BWV 126 (Sexagesimae)	MM
Herr Jesu Christ, wahr' Mensch und Gott, BWV 127 (Estomihi)	MM, PW
Du wahrer Gott und Davids Sohn, BWV 23 (Estomihi)	PW
Sehet! Wir gehn hinauf gen Jerusalem, BWV 159 (Estomihi)	JEG, MM, PW
Wie schön leuchtet der Morgenstern, BWV 1 (Maria Verkündigung)	JEG, PW
Himmelskönig, sei willkommen, BWV 182 (Palmarum)	JEG, PW
Christ lag in Todes Banden, BWV 4 (1. Osterfeiertag)	JEG, MM, PW
Der Himmel lacht, BWV 31 (1. Osterfeiertag)	JEG, PW
Bleib bei uns, denn es will Abend werden BWV 6 (2. Osterfeiertag)	JEG, MM
Halt im Gedächtnis Jesum Christ, BWV 67 (Quasimodogeniti)	MM
Weinen, Klagen, Sorgen, Zagen, BWV 12 (Jubilate)	JEG, MM, PW
Ihr werdet weinen und heulen, BWV 103 (Jubilate)	JEG, MM, PW
Wir müssen durch viel Trübsal, BWV 146 (Jubilate)	JEG, MM, PW

Cantata	Selected by
Sie werden euch in den Bann, BWV 44 (Exaudi)	PW
Erschallet, ihr Lieder, BWV 172 (1. Pfingstfeiertag)	PW
Also hat Gott die Welt geliebet, BWV 68 (2. Pfingstfeiertag)	JEG
Gelobet sei der Herr, BWV 129 (Trinitatis)	PW
Die Elenden sollen essen, BWV 75 (1. So. n. Trin.)	JEG, MM
O Ewigkeit, du Donnerwort, BWV 20 (1. So. n. Trin.)	MM, PW
Brich dem Hungrigen dein Brot, BWV 39 (1. So. n. Trin.)	JEG, MM, PW
Die Himmel erzählen die Ehre Gottes, BWV 76 (2. So. n. Trin.)	PW
Ich hatte viel Bekümmernis, BWV 21 (3. So. n. Trin.)	MM, PW
Ach, Herr, mich armen Sünder, BWV 135 (3. So. n. Trin.)	PW
Christ unser Herr zum Jordan kam, BWV 7 (Johannistag)	JEG
Freue dich, erlöste Schar, BWV 30 (Johannistag)	JEG
Vergnügte Ruh, BWV 170 (6. So. n. Trin.)	MM
Es ist dir gesagt, Mensch, BWV 45 (8. So. n. Trin.)	JEG
Herr, gehe nicht ins Gericht, BWV 105 (9. So. n. Trin.)	JEG, MM, PW
Schauet doch und sehet, BWV 46 (10. So. n. Trin.)	PW
Nimm von uns, Herr, BWV 101 (10. So. n. Trin.)	JEG, MM, PW
Herr, deine Augen, sehen nach dem Glauben, BWV 102 (10. So. n. Trin.)	PW
Mein Herze schwimmt im Blut, BWV 199 (11. So. n. Trin.)	MM, PW
Siehe zu, dass deine Gottesfurcht, BWV 179 (11. So. n. Trin.)	PW
Allein zu dir, Herr Jesu Christ, BWV 33 (13. So. n. Trin.)	PW
Jesu, der du meine Seele, BWV 78 (14. So. n. Trin.)	JEG, MM, PW
Es ist nichts Gesundes an meinem Leibe, BWV 25 (14. So. n. Trin.)	PW
Jauchzet Gott in allen Landen, BWV 51 (15. So. n. Trin.)	JEG
Liebster Gott, wenn werd ich sterben, BWV 8 (16. So. n. Trin.)	PW
Wer weiß, wie nahe mir mein Ende, BWV 27 (16. So. n. Trin.)	JEG, MM, PW
Christus, der ist mein Leben, BWV 95 (16. So. n. Trin.)	MM, PW
Komm, du süße Todesstunde, BWV 161 (16. So. n. Trin.)	PW
Es erhub sich ein Streit, BWV 19 (Michaelistag)	JEG, MM, PW
Herr Gott, dich loben alle wir, BWV 130 (Michaelistag)	PW
Wer sich selbst erhöhet, BWV 47 (17. So. n. Trin.)	PW
Gott soll allein mein Herze haben, BWV 169 (18. So. n. Trin.)	JEG, PW
Ich will den Kreuzstab gerne tragen, BWV 56 (19. So. n. Trin.)	JEG, MM, PW
Wo soll ich fliehen hin, BWV 5 (19. So. n. Trin.)	JEG
Ich elender Mensch, BWV 48 (19. So. n. Trin.)	JEG, PW
Schmücke dich, o liebe Seele, BWV 180 (20. So. n. Trin.)	MM, PW
Ein feste Burg ist unser Gott, BWV 80 (Reformationsfest)	JEG, PW
Ich armer Mensch, ich Sündenknecht, BWV 55 (22. So. n. Trin.)	JEG
Mache dich, mein Geist, bereit, BWV 115 (22. So. n. Trin.)	JEG, PW
O Ewigkeit, du Donnerwort, BWV 60 (24. So. n. Trin.)	PW
Wachet auf, ruft uns die Stimme, BWV 140 (27. So. n. Trin.	JEG, MM, PW

Figure 1.1. The 30 Best Cantatas (Sir John Eliot Gardiner, Michael Maul, Peter Wollny).

On the basis of our "hit parades", I drew up the rankings and was amazed to find that in 15 cases we all regarded the same work as indispensable, and there were many more matches (Figure 1).

The question of which pieces were ultimately to feature on the program—especially in those cases where we were not all of one opinion—was settled easily enough when I realised there was only one sensible way of deciding the order of the cantatas, and that was to group them according to their place in the church year, starting with the 1st Sunday in Advent and ending with Eternity Sunday. So the cycle begins, as befits such a large-scale work, with "Nun komm, der Heiden Heiland", BWV 61, in which, in the opening chorus, Bach clothes the familiar Luther chorale in the raiment of a French overture. It ends two days later with a—doubtlessly unnecessary—wake-up call: "Wachet auf, ruft uns die Stimme", BWV 140. Since the performance describes the full circle of the church year, and the entire cycle encompasses 18 hours of music, the obvious solution for naming this mammoth project was to borrow the name of the tetralogy by another great Leipzig composer and call it the "Ring of Cantatas" (For a full description of the cycle see Gardiner/Maul 2018).

The performance of the "Ring" was a huge success; tickets sold out quickly. People from more than 46 countries visited the "Ring", and the cycle received enthusiastic reviews from many of the most important journals and newspapers including the New York Times (June 15 and June 22) and many of Europe's leading media.

Despite the fact that I have been quite familiar with Bach's cantatas for almost two decades, the performance of the Leipzig "Ring" was also a very special and enlightening experience for me. I already knew that Bach's cantatas provide a wide variety of forms, musical experiments and breathtaking moments, and that their overall quality doesn't rank far below the quality of Bach's Passions or his B-minor Mass. However, what I learned while hearing all of these stunning performances by Suzuki, Koopman and Gardiner and seeing the frenetic applause of the international audience was that Bach's cantatas obviously represent the very heart of his art. Though originally composed as occasional works for a certain Sunday, a certain church and a certain congregation—many of them written under the constant pressure of time on a weekly basis—they are simply breathtaking masterworks providing all kinds of the musical art and features Bach is famous for. In order to prove this claim, I want to focus on several cantatas, comprising of pieces from Bach's early Mühlhausen and Weimar period to his mature Leipzig work. I want to point to some innovations with regards to word-painting, the relationship between text and music and intermingling musical genres and styles. Don't expect literally new discoveries. I only want to demonstrate that it's always worthwhile to dive deep into the fascinating world of J. S. Bach's cantatas.

Two early masterworks

We all know the old saying: No one is born a master. No doubt, that was right even in the case of Bach. Being an orphan in the age of 9, he apparently managed—supported by his teachers, Bach's brother, the Ohrdruf Organist Johann Christoph Bach and the Lüneburg organist Georg Böhm, and by inspiring role models such as the Hamburg organist Johann Adam Reincken and the Lübeck organist Dietrich Buxtehude—to become a fully-trained, brilliant organist and composer of organ music already at the age of about 18. In any event, he was appointed at this time—in August 1703—organist at the New Church in Arnstadt, Thuringia.

For the next five years, his work was mainly focused on playing the organ in the service, improvising all kinds of chorale arrangements, preludes, fugues and other kinds of organ genres. At the same time, he didn't show any particular interest in the regular performances of figural music during the services. According to some archival documents, he at least actively refused to take part in the Sunday's performances with the boys from the Arnstadt school choir and orchestra (Wolff, 2000, pp. 77–101).

Some Bach scholars, however, have argued for decades that at least one existing Bach cantata must have been composed already during Bach's Arnstadt period: the cantata "Nach dir, Herr, verlanget mich", BWV 150. Other scholars, including Joshua Rifkin, consider BWV 159 a spurious composition (Schulze, 2010, pp. 69–74). Preserved only in a copy from the late 1750s (D-B, P 1044), the textual structure of this piece and its musical style represent a composition that in all likelihood must have been composed at the turn of the eighteenth century. Therefore, in the case Bach were the composer, it would have been written very early in Bach's life, namely during his Arnstadt period. Thanks to the observation of the Belgian internet blogger Johan de Wael, who realized that each of the first letters of the four last lines of the last choir—to be read top down—represent the name BACH, the problems of authenticity and dating the composition were solved very recently. Identifying some minor mistakes, the copyist of the manuscript made when transcribing the text of the cantata, the Bach scholar Hans-Joachim Schulze figured out, that all the freely-invented texts of the cantata—apart from the movements based on biblical words—represent an acrostic. Reading the first letters of all the verses top down, the name of "DOKTOR CONRAD MECKBACH" appears (Schulze, 2010).

Meckbach was mayor in Mühlhausen when Bach was appointed the new Mühlhausen organist at Divi Blasii church in May 1707. Close to Bach's audition in Mühlhausen, Meckbach celebrated his 70th birthday—apparently the reason for Bach's wanting to impress the mayor with this cantata as a special birthday gift. In short, due to these new observations one can assume that cantata BWV 150 was composed in 1707 right at the moment when Bach left Arnstadt for Mühlhausen and apparently didn't have any pertinent experience in composing vocal music.

Despite Bach's apparent lack of extensive experience in this field, cantata 150 can by no means considered to be the composition of a freshman. For example, the center of the cantata provides a setting of Psalm 25, verse 5: "Leite mich in Deiner Wahrheit und lehre mich; denn du bist der Gott, der mir hilft, täglich harre ich Dein!" (Lead me in your Truth and teach me; for you are the God, who helps me, I await you daily).

In order to demonstrate musically the journey of a believer to heaven, who is constantly guided and taught by god, Bach came up with a striking idea of word painting, brilliantly realized in his score. The four singers plus the two violins are singing and playing repeatedly the words "Leite mich" all in all six times before ending the sentence with "in Deiner Wahrheit". At the same time, starting in the beginning in the bass, ending after six bars in the first violin three octaves higher, a constantly ascending scale in quarter notes, played by each of the voices alternatively in order of their pitch range, moves straight towards heaven.

With these seven bars, Bach composed a very moving musical picture and was able to heighten the impact of the words greatly. But again, it is hard to believe that this was the work of a beginner (piece fully described in Dürr, 2005, pp. 773–776; see also Wolff, 2000, pp. 100–101).

In Mühlhausen Bach's daily work was focused mainly on playing the organ. However, at least three more cantatas must have been composed during his only one-year tenure in the West-Thuringian city. All of the three cantatas provide impressive movements where Bach combined freely invented aria or choral melodies with chorale tunes so as to speak counterpart. The idea of combining a chorale with other (mostly biblical) texts and independent melodies was not an innovation created by Bach himself. It goes back to composers such as Heinrich Schütz (see part III of his "Musicalische Exequien": "Herr, nun lässest du deinen Diener fahren" SWV 281) and was very common in Thuringian motets from the late seventeenth century including pieces by J. S. Bach's relatives Johann Michael Bach and Johann Christoph Bach. However, in their pieces, the combination often sounds artificial or less-organic, and many composers try to avoid playing both melodies actually simultaneously. By contrast, the way the Mühlhausen Johann Sebastian Bach was able to combine a freely invented aria melody with chorale melodies was, in terms of intricacy, far from what his ancestors had achieved. The most notable example of this particular skill one can find is in the so-called "Actus tragicus" BWV 106, a piece composed on the occasion of a funeral of an unknown person, particularly in a fugue in the middle of the piece, sung on words from the Old Testament: "Es ist der alte Bund, Mensch du musst sterben" (It is the old covenant, man, you must die)—a three-part choral movement for alto, tenor and bass.

The question of why the choir surprisingly lacks the soprano is answered after the fugue theme goes through all the three voices twice. Now, suddenly, the soprano comments with a sentence from Revelation, chapter 20: "Ja, komm, Herr Jesu!" (Yes, come, Lord Jesus). The soprano expresses that nobody need be afraid of death because a Christian knows that Jesus, the Redeemer, will save his soul. Bach emphasizes this basic trust of every Christian with a special musical artifice: after a few bars of the soprano solo, the two *viola da gamba* start to accompany the soprano with an independent melodic line. More precisely, both instruments are playing a specific comment instrumentally, since the warm sounds of the violas are nothing more than phrases from the hitherto well-known chorale, "Ich hab mein Sach Gott heimgestellt", a song that deals with the yearning for salvation from the earthly vale [wähl] of tears. Verse 5 of the hymn says, "Today we are fresh, healthy and strong, but tomorrow we are lying dead in the coffin; Today we bloom like roses red, soon sick and dead."

In the last section of this dialogue between the soprano and the two violas, Bach notches up his performance in terms of skillfulness. What happens here makes the "Actus tragicus" that unique masterpiece many people see it as. Now Bach succeeds in combining all three elements of the movement: first the aforementioned transience, based on the Old testament and portrayed in the 3-part-choir; second the desire of the dying person for salvation, sung by the soprano with words from the Revelation; and third the instrumentally recited chorale melody. The three elements sound one after another and next to each other, they comment and condition each other. As a result, the complex picture of a death scene emerges in which an imaginary community stands around the deathbed and accompanies with chorales and words from the Old Testament an apparently female person struggling with death while she is preparing for her transition. Its highlight is a last appearance of the choral fugue theme. In the meantime, it has been modified in such a way that it reminds of the funeral song "Herzlich tut mich verlangen nach einem seel'gen End!" (I long for a happy ending). While choir and instruments fade out more and more, the dying person—briefly still accompanied by the pulse-like beat of the basso continuo—has her last breaths. And literally with the very last exhale of air and the name of her redeemer on her lips, she leaves the world.

After this, there is only silence. Bach demands a full stop with a fermata. This is without any doubt one of the most impressive pauses in music history—afterwards, in the second part of the piece, the soul awakes on her way to paradise (piece fully described in Duerr, 2006, pp. 758–765).

One of the many astonished listeners of the "Actus tragicus" should have a say, namely the 29-year-old Fanny Hensel née Mendelssohn-Bartholdy. In a letter to her brother Felix from November 1834, she wrote about the concluding passage of the first part of "Actus tragicus":

> "This afternoon I played two trios [...] by Carl Gottlieb Reißiger and George Onslow [...] but it was so dull, lame, fundamentally boring stuff that I almost got moldy when playing through, and then as a recuperation I played my favorite motet: 'Gottes Zeit ist die allerbeste Zeit'. Ah!! It will be good again. I do not know any more convincing preacher than the old Bach. If he climbs the pulpit in an aria, he does not leave his subject until he has thoroughly shaken or built and convinced his church. I almost do not know anything more beautiful than the passage 'It is the old covenant', to which the sopranos are so touchingly singing: 'Come, Lord Jesus, come'. Sebastian, not Bach, takes the pen out of my hand!"
>
> "*Heut Nachmittag spielte ich 2 Trios durch [...] von Reißiger u. Onslow. Es war aber so mattes, lahmes, grundlangweiliges Zeug, daß ich im Durchspielen fast verschimmelte, u. nachher zur Erholung die Litaney u. meine Lieblingsmotette: Gottes Zeit, spielte. Ah!! Dabei wird einem wieder wohl. Ich kenne keinen eindringlicheren Prediger als den alten Bach. Wenn er so in einer Arie die Kanzel besteigt, u. sein Thema nicht eher verläßt, bis er seine Gemeinde durch u. durch erschüttert oder erbaut u. überzeugt hat. Schöneres kenne ich fast nicht, als das Furchtbare ‚es ist der alte Bund', wozu die Soprane so rührend einstimmen: ja komm Herr Jesu! komm. Sebastian nicht Bach nimmt mir die Feder aus der Hand.*" (Bach-Dokumente VI, pp. 280–281).

A Weimar experiment

After serving for six years as organist at the court of Sachsen-Weimar Bach was promoted Concertmaster of the court chapel with the new obligation to compose sacred cantatas "all four weeks". Starting in March 1714 Bach created on a monthly basis new cantatas—about 20 pieces from the Weimar period have survived. In many of these cantatas Bach came up with stunning musical innovations and a musical style that sounds rather like compositions of a cosmopolitan Kapellmeister familiar with the musical map of the entirety of Europe rather than pieces of a musician who—as Bach in fact was—ranked only on the third position among the Weimar musicians (see the introduction into Bach's Weimar cantatas in Wolff, 2000, pp. 147–174). A famous example for Bach's, so to say, international approach is the cantata "Nun komm, der Heiden Heiland", BWV 61, composed for the first Sunday of Advent in 1714—in other words: the piece that musically provided the opener of the new church year. In order to demonstrate the character of inauguration of the church year, Bach presented an astonishing and striking idea that mingles characteristic elements of secular court music with a very traditional element of protestant church music. The opening movement of the cantata is surprisingly modeled after the Ouverture of a French Opera in pure Lully style. However, after a few bars, Bach combines the theme and the form of the Ouverture with the famous chorale "Nun komm der Heiden Heiland" by Martin Luther composed in the Dorian mode. The basic form of the ouverture, slow–fast (fugue)–slow, is maintained throughout the entire movement.

The orchestra starts with a quotation of the first chorale line in the instrumental bass, after which the same line is sung by all four voices in turn against the ceremonial dotted rhythms of the instruments. Line 2 follows in a chordal texture of voices. In the quick fugato of line 3, the instruments double the choir unisono, but line 4, returning to the style of line 2, is heard chordally within the solemn instrumental texture. What an ingenious combination of a chorale arrangement and a French Overture, perfectly demonstrating the character of the piece as an opener of the church year and representing music that overcomes the traditional borders between sacred and secular music (see the description of the entire cantata in Duerr, 2005, pp. 75–77).

Experiments in Bach's Leipzig *Cantata* cycles

Starting May 30, 1723 Bach served as the music director of Leipzig and the cantor of St. Thomas School—a boarding school which starting in the early seventeenth century was considered the most capable music school in entire protestant Germany given the cantor was allowed to choose his 54 students by testing them in a difficult musical entrance exam (on the genesis of Bach's St. Thomas School see Maul, 2018).

Bach's main business as Thomascantor was to perform sacred cantatas on a weekly basis in the Sunday or feast day services. These pieces, performed in-between the reading from the gospel and the sermon, were considered a musical sermon as their texts represented an interpretation or a commentary to the Sunday's readings.

About 150 sacred cantatas from Bach's Leipzig period have survived. After decades of a systematic evaluation of the sources, it has become clear that almost all of these pieces must have been composed during Bach's first four Leipzig years. Bach scholarship used to distinguish between three so-called annual cantata cycles (Jahrgänge), each of them providing pieces for any relevant Sunday and feast day of the church year.

Among the pieces Bach performed in his first Leipzig cycle—consisting of 55 cantatas—38 pieces were new compositions; the remaining cantatas were actually just re-performed pieces from Bach's Weimar period. It is characteristic for Bach's first Leipzig cycle that the cantatas can hardly be pressed into a binding form. This is particularly evident in the opening choirs. Often, they are structured in two parts, representing the form of a rather free prelude-like part followed by a strict fugue—a pattern that was not alien to the former organist J. S. Bach. Sometimes, however, Bach crosses the borders between the three usually independently used genres of chorus, aria and recitative (general introduction into Leipzig cycle I in Duerr, 2005, pp. 22–29; see also Wolff, 2000, pp. 268–275).

Christus, der ist mein Leben BWV 95

A very impressive example is the opening movement of the cantata "Christus, der ist mein Leben, Sterben ist mein Gewinn" (Christ is my life, death is my reward), BWV 95, written for the 16th Sunday after Trinity.

The reading text for that day is the awakening of the dead youth of Nain from the Gospel of Luke (7:14), one of the most spectacular miracles Jesus ever performed. Therefore, in the protestant music and the sermons created for this Sunday, the texts often display the yearning of a Christian to die in order to meet Jesus as soon as possible.

The opening chorus of Bach's cantata begins with a colorful concerto movement for two *oboe d'amore*, into which Bach inserted the well-known funeral chorale "Christus der ist mein Leben" by Melchior Vulpius, effectively ennobled with tonal expansions and changes to the melody of the chorale. After performing the first stanza, Bach comes up with a surprise: a solo tenor suddenly enters the instrumental concert, enthusiastically expressing his strong wish to die today rather than tomorrow. This happens first in a kind of arioso which, however, turns more and more into a secco recitative sparingly accompanied by the oboes with musical gestures of the beginning. Over the course of this recitative, the singer announces that his death song has already been composed, and that he is only waiting for the starting shot to sing it—a perfect announcement for Bach, since as a reaction he let the city pipers spontaneously intonate the most famous of all Lutheran funeral songs in a kind of jam session. The choir, which in the meantime had disappeared, finally enters the stage again singing this song with full conviction—and by doing so Bach gives us the chance to hear how the dying man is singing himself "mit Fried und Freud"—with peace and joy—towards the paradise. What a stroke of genius: an opening choral movement that playfully connects two chorales through an arioso and recitative in between, and at the same time offers a self-contained opening scene of the cantata, which provides in a really touching way the quintessence of the text of the gospel (see the description of the entire cantata in Duerr, 2005, pp. 546–550).

Wie zittern und Wanken from BWV 105

Besides experimental forms in the choral movements in his first Leipzig cycle, Bach also offers spectacular ideas of how to create arias representing the full scale of emotions—among them, there are numerous touching, even meditative moments. Such is the soprano aria "Wie zittern und wanken" from the cantata "Herr, Gehe nicht ins Gericht", BWV 105, composed in July 1723 for the 9th Sunday after Trinity. The aria is one of the few examples in which Bach used the so-called Bassettchen technique (Bassetto-technique), which is: to compose a piece without using basso continuo instruments, in other words: without a solid bass.

The gospel text of the Sunday is Jesus' parable of the unjust steward. Consequently, the unknown librettist tries to work out in the cantata how the principle of profit maximization can be combined with the Christian rules of life and thus tackles a hot topic in the rich trading city of Leipzig. Bach also took part in this brainwashing. In the archaic entrance choir, he composed for all those sinners a heavily sounding warning and let them literally plead for mercy before God. The fact that in the following aria he used the Bassetto-technique was not an arbitrary decision, but a well-fitting musical metaphor of the world, described in the cantata text: a world that has lost its fundaments, which are represented in the holy commandments from the Bible. At the same time, Bach painted in music the bewitching beauty of money. But that is, of course, a deceptive beauty. Since this was known at heart to all those Leipzig usurers and profiteers, Bach constantly underscores the magical interplay between soprano and oboe with repeated sixteenth notes in the high strings—a striking illustration of the constant trembling and staggering of the sinners which is described in the aria text (see also Duerr, 2005, pp. 464–467).

Herr Jesu Christ, wahr'r Mensch und Gott BWV 127

In his second Leipzig cycle, the so-called "Chorale Cantatas Cycle", Bach followed consistently the same approach. Week by week, he composed a cantata based on a certain church hymn. In the opening chorus, he presents the chorale melody nestled in a motetto-like polyphonic vocal setting, framed and decorated by an obligato orchestral part. In the recitatives and arias of a chorale cantata, the melody and the text of the several chorale stanzas are more or less present; however, in the final chorus, the last chorale stanza is sung in a plain four-voice setting. Starting the first Sunday after Trinity 1724—with an opening cantata that again started with the combination of a French ouverture and a chorale setting—Bach composed new cantatas on a weekly basis for almost nine months. However, for an unknown reason, he stopped the cycle at the end of February 1725 (general introduction into Leipzig cycle II in Duerr, 2005, pp. 29–36; see also Wolff, 2000, pp. 275–281).

In the last cantata of the cycle, “Herr Jesu Christ, wahr'r Mensch und Gott”, BWV 127, which was composed for the Sunday Estomihi (the last Sunday before Lent), Bach demonstrated in the opening chorus that for him the sky was not the limit, so to say. Different from what he had done in the previous cantatas, he worked not with only one hymn melody in the opening chorus of this piece. The cantata is based on the hymn “Herr Jesu Christ, wahr'r Mensch und Gott” by Paul Eber. It's a funeral hymn where in the first stanza the text refers to Jesus' passion and death on the cross. In the opening movement of Bach's cantata, however, Bach combines Paul Eber's hymn with a text-less presentation of the Lutheran Agnus Dei (“Christe, Du Lamm Gottes”)—and as if that were not enough, there are also several references in the basso continuo part to the Passion chorale “O Haupt voll Blut und Wunden”.

In other words, by using two further hymns as additional melodies or better counterthemes in his setting of “Herr Jesu Christ, wahr’r Mensch und Gott”, Bach is able to refer musically to the dualism of God and man and the relationship of the individual believer to Christ’s cross and Christ’s passion (description of the piece in Duerr, 2005, pp. 247–248).

Today, ordinary listeners of that piece don’t realize the complexity of the movement and the appearance of one, partly two additional chorale melodies and their meaning as they are usually not familiar with the melodies anymore. However, for Bach's contemporaries, the meaning must have been obvious. To make the complexity and the presence of additional chorale melodies apparent, John Eliot Gardiner decided on a radical step. When he performed BWV 127 during his Bach pilgrimage in 2000, an additional choir sang *colla parte* the instrumental parts playing the German Agnus Dei. The effect was simply breathtaking (live recording from Cambridge, King’s College Chapel, 5 March 2000. Label Soli Deo Gloria, SDG 118).

“Listen, play, love, revere–and keep your trap shut!”

The more we dive into the world of Bach’s sacred cantatas with their characteristics, special features and innovations, the more humbled and impressed we are. To be sure, almost all of his cantatas were nothing but “occasional music”, composed for a particular Sunday and a specific Lutheran congregation, and there were other contemporaries such as Georg Philipp Telemann, Christoph Graupner, Gottfried Heinrich Stölzel or Johann Friedrich Fasch, who over the course of years or even decades, put down on paper sacred cantatas of high musical quality on a weekly basis. But the widespread enthusiasm for Bach's sacred cantatas, which today—as the Leipzig "Ring of Cantatas" has shown—is a global phenomenon, proves impressively that Bach has created a timeless repertoire that meanwhile overcomes even religious borders. Without wanting to disparage the cantatas of Bach's contemporaries, it would be difficult to find parallel examples in Western cultural history where under such great pressure of time and over such a long time period a large body of work of comparable artistry was created. Especially Bach's Leipzig cantatas are simply masterpieces produced on a weekly basis–all of them composed on an unbelievably high artistic and intellectual level and under circumstances that do not fit into our picture of a masterpiece on which the genius painstakingly works for months or even years before it finally comes to perfection.

Bach's phenomenon becomes totally mysterious if we realize that his weekly cantata production, which kept him busy during his first four Leipzig years, was not the only artistic outcome of this period. At the same time Bach was also able to compose milestones in music history such as his Magnificat (probably in summer 1723), his St. John Passion (first version Good Friday 1724) and his St. Matthew Passion (probably Good Friday 1727). At this point, it is not necessary to emphasize the outstanding art Bach demonstrated in these particular compositions. Here, too, Bach constantly led his interpreters to the limits of the possible—and sometimes beyond. And here, too, the amount of creative ideas and intricate compositional witchcraft is breathtaking, but never an end in itself. Rather, Bach challenges listeners at various levels to seek out the subtle connections between theological and musical messages. This happens in these pieces to the extent that some Bach enthusiasts of posterity started to call Bach the "Fifth Evangelist" (first done by Swedish archbishop Nathan Söderblom in 1929) or the "God's Gleeman" (Wilibald Gurlitt) (Sandberger, 1997, p. 11).

But in the end, Bach's cantatas are not inferior in terms of artistry. All the more, it is difficult to understand how Bach was able to deliver musical reflections on the Gospel texts at such a high level on a weekly basis over such a long period of time. Obviously, during the first three decades of his life he developed a compositional craftmanship, which enabled him in an unprecedented way to recognize quickly the polyphonic options of a musical theme and how to develop it in a, so to say, auto-pilot mode while demonstrating an unmistakable sense for phrasing, text declamation, word painting and proportions.

Today, we can only be astonished by these skills and at best can try to understand how the "Evangelist" Bach made almost all of his cantatas thrilling musical sermons on the Sunday's readings. But we may never properly explain or understand his genius. And so, given the inscrutable beauty and diversity of Bach's cantatas, we may certainly agree with Albert Einstein. Once asked by a German journal about his relationship to Bach, the great physicist, who spent his life searching for no more and no less than the formula of the universe, had a very clear recommendation: "This is what I have to say about Bach: listen, play, love, revere—and keep your trap shut!" ("Was ich zu Bachs Lebenswerk zu sagen habe: Hören, spielen, lieben, verehren und—das Maul halten!"; answer given to the weekly journal "Reclams Universum", 24 March 1929; see Steiner, 2005, p. 204.).

References

Bach Dokumente VI (2007), Ausgewählte Dokumente zum Nachwirken Johann Sebastian.

Bachs 1801–1850. *Herausgegeben und erläutert von Andreas Glöckner, Anselm Hartinger und Karen Lehmann* (Johann Sebastian Bach. Neue Ausgabe sämtlicher Werke. Supplement VI). Kassel: Bärenreiter-Verlag.

Dürr, L. (2005). *The Cantatas of J. S. Bach.* Oxford: Oxford University Press.

Gardiner/Maul (2018). *Leipziger Kantaten-Ring / Leipzig Ring of Cantatas, Freitag bis Sonntag, 8.–10. Juni 2018.* Leipzig: Bach-Archiv Leipzig.

Maul, M. (2018). *Bach's famous Choir – The Saint Thomas School in Leipzig, 1212–1804.* London: Boydell&Brewer.

Sandberger W. (1997). *Das Bach-Bild Philipp Spittas - Ein Beitrag zur Geschichte der Bach-Rezeption im 19. Jahrhundert - Beihefte zum Archiv für Musikwissenschaft, XXXIX.* Stuttgart: Franz Steiner Verlag.

Schulze, H.-J. (2010). "Rätselhafte Auftragswerke Johann Sebastian Bachs", in *Bach-Jahrbuch 2010,* pp. 69–93. Leipzig: Evangelische Verlagsanstalt.

Steiner, F. (2005). "Einsteins kosmische Religiosität", in Frank Steiner (Ed.), *Albert Einstein: Genie, Visionär und Legende,* pp. 191–218. Heidelberg: Springer.

Wolff C. (2000). *Johann Sebastian Bach. The Learned Musician.* New York: W.W. Norton.

Chapter 2

From Bach's violin to Italian pianos: the *Sei Solo* in the Italian piano transcriptions

by Chiara Bertoglio

Conservatory of Music of Cuneo, Italy

To trace the history of the reception of Bach in Italy means to create a narrative encompassing the public and semi-public performances of his works, the critical discussions of such performances and of individual works, the publications and editions of his works, the audio and video recordings when available, but also the creative engagements with his output, in the form of transcriptions, arrangements, paraphrases, *hommages à Bach* and similar works.[1] In this article, I will focus my attention on transcriptions from Bach's *Sei Solo* for the violin having the piano (two hands) as their instrument of destination, discussing their approach, their relationships (when these are discernible) and their main features.

Transcriptions of Bach's works have been realized by Bach himself; indeed, several movements of the *Sonatas and Partitas* were reworked by Bach for other instrumental media or groups. In detail, the Fugue from *Sonata I* became the Organ Fugue BWV 539 and the Lute Fugue BWV 1000; the *Sonata II* was transcribed for keyboard as BWV 964; the Adagio from the *Sonata III* is found in a keyboard transcription (transposed to G major) in the *Clavierbüchlein für Wilhelm Friedemann Bach* (listed as BWV 968, and possibly attributable to Wilhelm Friedemann Bach himself); the entire *Partita III* is listed as BWV 1006A for the lute, though it is playable only on the keyboard's *Lautenwerk*; the Prelude from the same Partita also became the

[1] I wish to express my gratitude to my colleague Dr. Maria Borghesi, to Prof. Dario Lo Cicero, to Prof. Riccardo Risaliti and to Prof. Patrizia Romano for their kind help in the process of research leading to this article.

Symphony for Cantata BWV 29 (*Wir danken dir, Gott, wir danken dir*), in a D-major setting for organ and orchestra.

In the nineteenth century, the piano transcriptions by Franz Liszt unavoidably became the reference point for all later transcribers, along with those by Tausig; in 1878, Johannes Brahms realized masterly piano transcriptions of excerpts from the violin *Sonatas and Partitas*: significantly, they were published among his *Studies*, just as most reprints of Simrock's pioneering publication of the original violin works were titled *Studio o sia Tre Sonate per il Violino Solo*.

The first Italian name which comes to a musician and musicologist's mind when thinking of Bach transcriptions for the piano is, of course, that of Ferruccio Busoni (1866-1924); and one of the most famous and performed of his piano transcriptions is the *Chaconne* from *Partita II* (Bach 1893).[2] It was premiered by Busoni himself in Boston, on January 30th, 1893, and published soon thereafter; it also underwent new editions during the composer's lifetime (in 1902, 1907 and 1916). The concept underlying Busoni's transcription is markedly different from Brahms', and has been described by Busoni himself as follows:

> [In the] piano transcription of the Chaconne for violin [...] the editor has [...] treated tonal effects in an organistic sense. This procedure, which has been variously attacked, finds its justification chiefly in the meaningful content which cannot attain complete expression through the violin, and also in the example set by Bach in the characteristic organ transcription of his violin fugue in G minor.[3]

Here Busoni demonstrates his familiarity with Bach's oeuvre and with his transcription practices, while appealing to them in order to justify his own, very personal aesthetic concept on pseudo-historical grounds. The evident effort, embodied in the original *Chaconne*, to overcome the physical and technical limitations of the instrument legitimizes, in Busoni's view, not only the use of an instrument more naturally suited to polyphony, but also the full exploitation of the late Romantic piano's potential. On the other hand, however, Busoni seriously considered the violin performing traditions of his own era: as demonstrated by Paul Banks (1996), whereas other transcribers of the *Chaconne* took inspiration mainly from the accompaniments realized by

---

2 As concerns the transcriptions of Bach's *Chaconne*, see, for example, Feder 1969; Eiche 1985; on Busoni's version, see Fabrikant 2006.

3 As translated in Busoni 1894: 169.

Mendelssohn and/or Schumann, several of Busoni's interpretations of Bach's abbreviations reveal that one of his interpretive sources was the instructive edition realized by Ferdinand David for the violin.

If Busoni aimed at a piano version which could rival, in effect and in instrumental means, the difficulty and impressiveness of the violin original, the following Italian piano transcription revealed an entirely different approach. Sigismondo Cesi (1869-1936), whose musical lineage mounted back to Sigismund Thalberg (in whose honour he was Christened, and who was one of the apostles of the Bach-cult in Naples, one of the main Italian Bach-cities), included the Gavotte from *Partita III* in a collection of piano works, complementing the famous piano method he realized jointly with Ernesto Marciano (Cesi 1897). His transcription abounds in dynamic and articulation signs and is pianistically effective; in spite of its "educational" destination (revealed also in the trills' realization), it is more elaborate than Boschian's version,[4] though it has several elements in common with Mugellini's.[5]

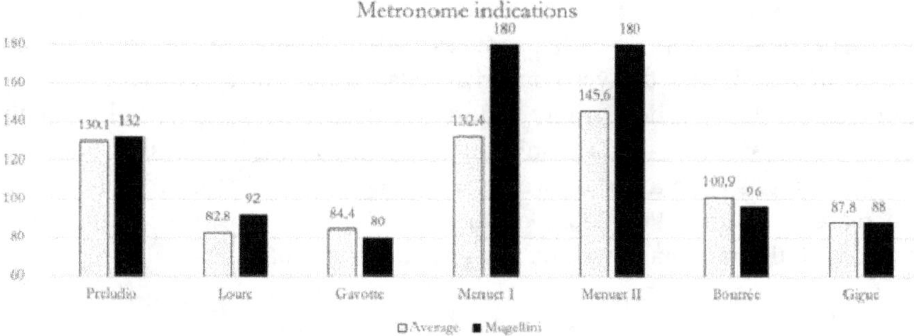

Figure 2.1. Metronome indications for Partita III.

Indeed, Bruno Mugellini's did not "transcribe" *Partita III.* As is well known, together with Egon Petri, he cooperated with Busoni in the realization of the "Busoni-Ausgabe", the interpretive edition of Bach's keyboard works—comprising instructive editions, arrangements and other forms of "written interpretations".[6] Volume 24 of the Busoni-Ausgabe (Mugellini 1921) comprises

[4] As regards Boschian, see later in this paper.

[5] For example, both are marked "Allegro moderato". Mugellini and Boschian indicate *Alla breve,* Cesi common time.

[6] Cf. Bertoglio 2012: 212-213 etc.

some "keyboard" works which had been included in the *Bach-Gesellschaft-Ausgabe*—the textual source used by Busoni and his co-editors. Thus, it also included the lute (or rather *Lautenwerk*) version of *Partita III*; this edition is provided with metronome indications, which are normally quicker than the average indications[7] of the violinists/editors.

Movements 2-6 of the *Partita* are provided with the indications of tempo, articulation, expression, dynamics, etc. usually found in instructive editions; the Prelude, however, is printed twice, once "in the original notation", i.e. with the notes and the original dynamic indications printed in conformity with the BGA (editorial additions are also found, but they are distinguishable from the "original" text), and in a "Variante (con adattamento tecnico moderno)" (a pianistic adaptation which in most cases involves a different distribution of the notes between the two hands). This second version was later reprinted, probably without the editor's or publisher's knowledge or authorization, by a Moscow company, in a volume comprising different "transcriptions" of this Prelude (Bach 1960) - thus, Mugellini was erroneously credited with a "transcription" of BWV 1006. However, interesting comparisons can be made as concerns the interpretive concept transmitted by his edition and that found in the transcription of the same Prelude published in 1921 by Riccardo Pick-Mangiagalli, in a diptych comprising also the Adagio from *Sonata I* (Pick-Mangiagalli 1921). The entirely different dynamic concept found in their versions is striking: as shown in Figure 2, while Pick-Mangiagalli builds up twice a dynamic climax, in the very same bars Mugellini prescribes a marked decrease in volume. Pick-Mangiagalli's transcription transforms the original work, with brilliant piano writing and a virtuoso approach.

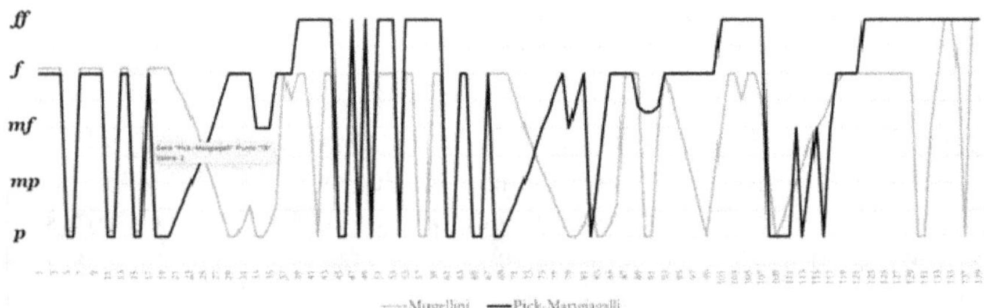

Figure 2.2. Dynamic indications (Bruno Mugellini and Riccardo Pick Mangiagalli), Prelude from Partita III.

[7] Average calculated on the basis of the data found in Papadopoulou (2015): 347-349.

Pick's transcription of the G-minor *Adagio* seems to be intended also as a Prelude to the other Prelude, and this appears to be the reason for its transposition to B minor. His late-Romantic approach, reminiscent of Busoni's organ-like concept, can be usefully compared with a later transcription of the same piece, in the original key, realized by Sergio Fiorentino (1927-1998) and recently published in a posthumous collection (Fiorentino 2011). The comparison can be made, however, only between "the notes" of the two versions, since—as stated by the editor,

> There were several versions for some of the pieces, and moreover they were different from how he actually played them, and nearly all lacked dynamic and phrasing indications, etc. I had to work on the originals in order to add those valuable indications. Sergio [...] only wrote down the notes, no other signs.[8]

Here too Pick-Mangiagalli's version is the most grandiose, virtuoso and majestic of the two, with octave doublings and a magniloquent style. If here the influence of Busoni is clearly discernible, in the case of another transcription (Bach 1953; first Double from *Partita I*), realized by the organist Alfredo Gattari (1894-1972), the style is clearly reminiscent of the two Brahmsian *Studies* on the G-minor *Presto*. As happened in Brahms's model, the broken arpeggios of the original are played by one hand, while the other fills the harmonic texture with similar formulae.

In more recent times, Angelo Boschian (b. 1951) has realized several piano transcriptions from, among others, numerous individual movements excerpted from the *Sonatas and Partitas*, including the Chaconne. The unusual choice to transcribe all of the violin Gavottes is part of a larger project by Boschian, comprising several other examples of this form found in Bach's oeuvre.[9] The less surprising choice of transcribing the Chaconne resulted in a

---

[8] Private communication via email, April 2nd, 2019. Fiorentino's practice is doubtless due to the fact that he was writing down "the notes" for his own use. As concerns the date of realization of these transcriptions, Risaliti was not able to give information, though he stated that "some of the transcriptions" had been realized at a very early date. However, I have found on a Russian website (http://bit.ly/fiorentinobach, last accessed June 27th, 2019) a copy of Fiorentino's transcriptions which had not been scanned from Risaliti's edition; it was typeset with Finale, and thus it is possible that it is a pirate copy of Fiorentino's own score. At the end of the Adagio, a small typewritten signature is found: "S. F.; 25/12/95*". It may be therefore that this particular transcription had not been realized (or typed) before 1995, and this is consistent with the fact that Fiorentino's own recording of this transcription was realized on 19/10/1996 at the Konzertsaal Siemensvilla in Berlin (copyright 1998 Appian, ASIN B000026AV2).

[9] Boschian's piano transcriptions of the Gavottes have been recorded and published in the CD *Promenade* by pianist Alessandro Cesaro (Rivoalto CRR2302).

version markedly different from Busoni's, with fewer technical difficulties, restrained harmonic fillings, and few added indications. It is interesting to observe, however, that Boschian follows Busoni and other earlier transcribers (rather than the violin text of the *Neue Bach Ausgabe*) in adopting triple-stopped chords in the first bars of the piece.[10]

In spite of their radical diversity, or perhaps by virtue of it, these numerous transcriptions and their chronology reveal an enduring and constant interest by Italian pianists and composers in Bach's *Sonatas and Partitas*, as well as their desire to engage artistically and creatively with them. The various styles, approaches and aesthetics reveal the historical changes in taste and perspective, as well as the individual transcribers' personality and different intended public and occasions of performance. Together, they create a mosaic and a narrative, which in turn contributes to the larger, and ever-evolving, picture of the reception of Bach in Italy.

Transcriptions

Bach, J. S. (1953). *Double (dalle sonate per Violino solo). Realizzazione di Alfredo Gattari.* Bologna: Bongiovanni, 1953. Plate number 2351.

Bach, J. S. (c. 1893). *Chaconne aus der vierten Sonate für Violine allein von Johann Sebastian Bach. Zum Concertvortrage für Pianoforte bearbeitet und Herrn Eugen d'Albert zugeeignet von Ferruccio B. Busoni.* Leipzig: Breitkopf & Härtel.

Bach, J. S. (1960). *Preljudija iz skripičnoj partity no 3; (Simfonija iz kantaty no 29) v avtorskoj klavirnoj redakcii i v obrabotkach dlja fortep'jano / I.S. Bach (1685-1750); B. Mudžellini, K. Rejneke, A. Rubbacha, S. Rachmaninova, A. Ziloti i K. Sen-Sansa; vstupitel'naja stat'ja, sostavlenie, redakcija i kommentarii L. I. Rojzamana.* Moscow: Gosudarstvennoe Muzykal'noe Izdatel'stvo.

Boschian, A. (n.d.). *Gavotte.* Padova: Armelin. SDP 018.

Boschian, A. (n.d.). *Bourrée e Double dalla Partita n. 1 per violino, BWV 1002; Largo dalla Sonata n. 3 per violino, BWV 1005.* Padova: Armelin. SDP 011.

Boschian, A. (n.d.). *Ciaccona dalla Partita n. 2 per violino BWV 1004.* Padova: Armelin. SDP 013.

Cesi, S., arr. (c. 1897). *Gavotta: (dalla sonata per violino) G. S. Bach; trascrizione di Sigismondo Cesi ("Biblioteca pianistica per la gioventù: seconda serie: a due mani / scritta, riveduta, accentata e diteggiata da Sigismondo Cesi e Ernesto Marciano").* Milan: Ricordi. 100769.

Fiorentino, S. (2011). *Trascrizioni da concerto per pianoforte. A cura di Riccardo Risaliti.* Milan: Curci. EC11724.

[10] Paul Banks suggested that this tradition could be traced back to David's edition for the violin. Cf. Banks 1996.

Mugellini, B., ed. (1921). *J. S. Bach. Klavierwerke. Busoni-Ausgabe. Band XXIV.* Leipzig: Breitkopf & Härtel. Nr. 4324, plate number 27470.

Pick-Mangiagalli, R. (1921). *Due preludii (dalle sonate per violin solo) / G. S. Bach; trascritti per pianoforte da Riccardo Pick Mangiagalli.* Milan: G. Ricordi e C. ER299.

References

Banks, P. (1996). "Busoni and Bach's Chaconne in the Nineteenth Century". In *Ninth Conference on Nineteenth Century Music.* [online]. Available at: https://pwb101.me.uk/busoni-and-bachs-chaconne-in-the-nineteenth-century [Accessed 13 June 2019].

Bertoglio, C. (2012). *Instructive Editions of Bach's* Wohltemperirtes Klavier*: An Italian Perspective.* PhD. The University of Birmingham (UK), Birmingham.

Busoni, F. (1894). "First Appendix". In F. Busoni, ed., *The Well-Tempered Clavichord, vol. 1, by Johann Sebastian Bach, revised, annotated, and provided with parallel examples and suggestions for the study of modern piano-forte technique by Ferruccio Busoni,* 1st ed. New York: G. Schirmer; Boston: Boston Music Co.; Leipzig: Fr. Hofmeister.

Eiche, J., ed. (1985). *The Bach Chaconne for Violin Solo: A Collection of Views.* Bloomington In Frangipani Press.

Fabrikant, M. (2006). *Bach-Busoni Chaconne. A piano transcription analysis.* PhD. The University of Nebraska, Lincoln.

Feder, G. (1969). "Geschichte der Bearbeitung von Bachs Chaconne". In M. Geck, ed., *Bach-Interpretation,* Göttingen: Vandenhoeck & Ruprecht, 168-189.

Papadopoulou, V. (2015). *Zur Editions- und Aufführungsgeschichte von J. S. Bachs Sonaten und Partiten für Violine solo in der Zeit von 1802 bis 1940.* PhD. Universität Wien, Vienna.

Chapter 3

Sonatas and *Partitas* for violin: a play of mediations

by Maria Borghesi

Hochschule für Musik Dresden, Germany

The reception phenomena can be conceived as a massive space built around a central core, here occupied by *Sonatas* and *Partitas* for solo violin by J. S. Bach. This three-dimensional place is traversed by unorganized forces that, in this case, represent three pairs of intertwined issues concerning destinations, functions, and approaches to the principal object. The twentieth-century Italian music context stays in the background.

Didactic *vs* performance

Since 1899 national programs prescribed young violinists to perform two movements from a *Sonata* or a *Partita* in their 'compimento medio'—the mandatory exam scheduled after eight years of study—and two complete works at the end of their ten-year educational path at the final *diploma.* In particular, the study of Bach's collection—together with Paganini's *Caprices*—represented an essential rite of passage from the former position of student to that of advanced *éleve* and young professional performer. Because of this crucial educational function, the Italian publishing market entrusted the editing of instructive editions to some of the most renown teachers and performers. The first one, edited by Ettore Pinelli in 1887, was explicitly published for the Liceo Musicale "Santa Cecilia" in Rome. A few decades later, in 1921, the Milanese Ricordi renewed its editorial catalogue by prosing a new volume by Marco Anzoletti. As Anzoletti wrote in the *Preface,* since the inclusion of the *Sonatas and Partitas* into the national Ministerial programs «it became necessary to provide students with a teaching text of these works» (Anzoletti 1921, p. 3).

Beginning with these premises, three main tendencies swayed the history of Italian editions of Bach's *Sei Solo* in the second half of the twentieth century. On the one side, editors progressively lost their focus on education, diminishing the didactic emphasis in instructive indications and enlarging the public to not-identifiable categories of performers. On the other, performative and didactic precedents proposed by Italian editors were progressively substituted performative models attested and widespread by most renown foreign virtuosos, mirroring the process of internationalisation of the musical taste (cf. Faticoni 1987). Finally, in the twentieth century, Italian publishers diminished investment in the continual updating of editions: after Pinelli's and Anzoletti's works, Ricordi printed a not-commented volume by Enrico Polo (1933), and an instructive edition by the famous virtuoso and teacher Mario Corti in 1949. Corti's work early disappeared from the market, but Enrico Polo's 1933 and Gioacchino Maglioni's 1956 editions still appeared in Ricordi's 1994-1995 catalogue, despite their editorial and performative criteria answered to out-of-date habits both on the aesthetical and scientific point of view. In the meantime, even other publishers neglected Bach's *Sei Solo:* Carisch and Curci only published an instructive edition (respectively by Poltronieri in 1946 and Abbadoin 1972); the Florentine publisher, S.P.E.S, printed an anastatic edition (1985); and Suvini Zerboni introduced in its catalogue a publication by the performer Franco Gulli in 2003. This neglect of Bach was singular by respect to the broader Italian reception phenomenon of him[1], and it arises two hypotheses. Firstly, Italian students may have rejected the use of Italian editions edited by Italian teachers, preferring to them the most qualified critical or Urtext versions. Secondly, the absence of performative publications may be due to lack of demand, Italian violinists abandoned Bach's *Sei Solo* after their education, declining to perform them professionally. Both these hypotheses suggest a chance in perspective by comparing matters shown by the examination of the educational and editorial contexts with the more extensive background of the Italian cultural reception of Bach and this outstanding violin collection.

Virtuosic piece *vs* monographic collection

Since their rediscovery in the nineteenth century, Bach's *Sonatas* and *Partitas* have played two different roles when played in concerts. Firstly, they were separated and performed in single movements: these extracts were played at the beginning of a 'historical concert' as an attestation of the former state of the violin art, or during the concert as virtuosic pieces showing the performer's technical and interpretative abilities. The most performed movement was the *Chaconne* from the *2nd Partita* BWV 1004, which

---

[1] We can take the example of the 'sister' collection of *Sonatas* and *Partitas*, the *Cello Suites* of which Italian publishers proposed new instructive (and Urtext) editions since the end of the 80s. (Cf. Borghesi 2019b)

represented a top of the violin solo-repertoire, and lived an independent fortune thanks to the number of transcriptions for solo monodic and polyphonic instruments, ensembles, and orchestras. Looking at concert programs of the most influential music seasons in Rome and Milan[2], the performance of separated and single movements was common until the post-First World War. Performers and institutions then progressively changed the format of concerts, privileging shorter events with a higher internal coherence. The *Chaconne* continued to be often performed as soloist piece in concerts with orchestras, or as an encore, until the 1970s. Secondly, the complete performance of a *Sonata* or a *Partita* was included in chamber-music recitals as single but coherent work. This practice had been imported and spread by foreign, internationally-renown violinists (such as Joseph Szigeti, Nathan Milstein, Henryk Szeryng, and—later—Yehudi Menuhin) who deeply influenced the local music taste in Italy by including it as a destination in their tours.

Since the economic and social reestablishment after the Second World War, stages of the most consolidated music institutions occasionally hosted monographic performances of Bach's *Sei Solo* opera omnia. The first couple of concerts date back to 1959 and to 1961, when Milstein proposed them at the Sala Verdi in the Milan Conservatoire. However, these were considered unique events only open to selected and trained audiences, as it was for the Società del Quartetto and its strict public of subscribers. In the following decades, the situations changed little: although more diffused, the *opera omnia* of Bach's *Sei Solo* remained an exceptional appointment in which only a few institutions invested. The Teatro alla Scala proposed the entire cycle of *Partitas* in 1976 and then the complete performance of both *Sonatas and Partitas* in 1985, by choosing to involve two important Italian violinists (Gulli and Accardo). The Società del Quartetto of Milan—after Milstein's experience—planned two further *opera omnia* in 1989 and 1994 (respectively by Miriam Fried, and by Mark Kaplan and Marco Rizzi). With regards to Rome, the Accademia Nazionale di Santa Cecilia planned a performance of *Sei Solo* by two Italian virtuosos (Accardo and Ughi) in 1985 and 1993. Meanwhile, the

[2] The research had been conducted by examining concert seasons from 1950 to 2000 of the following music institutions: Accademia Nazionale Santa Cecilia, Accademia Filarmonica Romana, and Istituzione Universitaria dei Concerti in Rome; Teatro alla Scala, Società del Quartetto, Pomeriggi Musicali, Angelicum, and Musica e Poesia a San Maurizio in Milan.

Accademia Filarmonica Romana included the complete series only once, by entrusting it to the German violinist Christian Tetzlaff[3].

To consolidate my hypotheses about the educational role of the *Sei Solo* and their editorial destination, it is essential to consider another question: did Italian violinists performed this collection (or extracts from it) in the most significant concert seasons? And, if so, who played it? Examination of concert programs reveals that, although performing a complete *Sonata* or *Partita* was not common compared to other keyboard pieces by Bach, the performance of these works by Italian violinists was incredibly rare[4]. Moreover, by examining those concerts by Italian violinists performing Bach, it is evident that most of them were performed by a strict group of virtuosi whose names often recurred (such as Gioconda De Vito, Giuliano Carmignola, Salvatore Accardo, and Uto Ughi)[5]. This engendered an extreme imbalance in favour of performances by (prominent) virtuosos coming from abroad, which is further accentuated if one looks at the discography market. During the second half of the twentieth century, we find in Italy integral recordings of Bach's *Sei Solo* for violin performed by more than twenty-five different interpreters. Among them, only three were Italians. Until the 1990s, the total number of recordings was limited to the *Partita n. 2* and its *Chaconne*. This is the case with Salvatore Accardo's complete performance recorded by Philips in 1976[6]. Before that, the Italian-British violinist De Vito recorded the *Partita n. 2* BWV 1004 and its *Chaconne* twice in 1947 and 1950 for La Voce del Padrone; RCA released Ughi's *Sonata and Partita nn. 2* BWV 1003 and 1004 in 1981; and Franco Gulli, instead, recorded the *Sonata n. 1* BWV 1001 in 1973 for the Italian label Angelicum. The situation slightly changed in the last decade of the century, when two other outstanding Italian virtuosos, Roberto Michelucci (Fonè 1988-1989)[7] and Uto Ughi (RCA 1991) recorded three complete cycles of the *Sonatas* and *Partitas*[8]. In brief, Italian violinists rarely recorded Bach's solo works: the

---

[3] Other institutions, such as I Pomeriggi Musicali and the Angelicum in Milan, or the Istituzione Universitaria dei Concerti (IUC) in Rome limited their offer to occasional performances of no more than a couple of consecutive violin solo-works.

[4] Only a third of concerts including at least a movement from a *Sonatas* and *Partitas* were executed by Italian violinists.

[5] Accardo and Ughi performed alone more than one third of concerts by Italian virtuosos.

[6] Accardo recorded for a second time all *Sonatas* and *Partitas* in 2007 for the Italian label Foné.

[7] Roberto Michelucci studied with Anzelotti and for a long time playing as the first violin of the Italian ensemble *I Musici* devoted to the performance of Baroque music on modern instruments.

[8] Ughi recorded *Sonatas* and *Partitas* in 2005 for the Italian label Stradivarius again.

interest of virtuosos was generally limited to the *Chaconne*, except for single interpreters already projected on the international scene.

By examining these data, it is possible to make two parallel and interconnected considerations: firstly, as I often remarked in my researches on the Italian phenomenon of Bach-reception, Italians rarely fixed their theoretical investigations and practical interpretations of Bach's music, whose comprehension was considered an exclusive mark of the German (or, at least, North-European) world (Borghesi 2019a). Secondly, a brief overview of the live music shows that this lack overpassed limits of discography and it also affected the much more volatile world of concert performances. Indeed, Italian violinists rarely approached *Sei Solo* professionally, except for the big international stars who performed them in Italy as well as abroad, embodying supranational trends, habits, and tastes.

Modernised interpretation *vs* HIP

A third conjuncture influencing the reception of Bach's *Sonatas* and *Partitas* concerns the performance practice. As said, this outstanding collection for violin has been included in the repertoire of the most virtuosic performers since the second half of the nineteenth century. Taste and techniques changed over the decades, so that following generations of virtuosos coped with the performance of these eccentric works by proposing a new broad variety of interpretations. That said, although performance practices varied across decades, in Italy performers continued to conceive Bach's *Sei Solo* on modern instruments by adopting a modern technique. In this sense, the marked connection between the performative and the educative destination of the *Sonatas* and *Partitas* legitimated and emphasized the validity of a traditional academic approach. In this regard, it is interesting to read what Salvatore Accardo stated in 1985 (on occasion of Bach's birth-tercentenary) about organological and performative issues connected to Bach's *Sei Solo*. Formerly, he smothered the discussion on the use of historical instruments by remarking that "for violinists the problem of the use of original instruments in the performance of early music is undoubtedly different than for others. Indeed, we use very original instruments, built in the eighteenth and nineteenth century ... Modifications—by which we take advantage today—undoubtedly ameliorated string-instruments providing a more powerful sound. Who can establish how people played at that time, and who can say if Bach would have preferred how we play today? If there has been progress, why not to take advantage of them?" Accardo continued his discourse stating that "Bach has to be performed without to misinterpret his art, but with great phantasy", and therefore without limiting the interpretation into the borders of an historically-informed ambitus (Lugaresi 1985, p. 60).

To conclude: starting from the 1970s, the *Sonatas* and *Partitas* entered in the domain of performers interested in the rediscovery of ancient instruments and in the study of historically-informed performance practices (cf. Fabian 2005; Fabian 2015, pp. 75-122, Fabian 2017). However, the story of Bach's *Sei Solo* in Italy showed again a substantial displacement in favour of Romantic and Classical modernised interpretations. Until 2000, the Italian discographic market offered only one performance of *Sonatas* and *Partitas* on the baroque violin (Kuijken 1981) and audiences could not hope to assist to historically informed concerts out of circles explicitly devoted to baroque music[9]. Finally, if we consider Accardo's statements, it seems that the search for a potential mediation between new and historically informed instances in performance practice was already very far from that small portion of Italian violinists interested in Bach's *Sei Solo*.

Editions of J. S. Bach's *Sonatas and Partitas* for unaccompanied violin

Abbado, Michelangelo (1943). Sei Solo. Sonate e tre Partite per violino. Revisione di Michelangelo Abbado. Milano: Curci. Ed. n. 9527.

Anzoletti, Marco (1921). Sonate e Partite per violino solo, rivedute e commentate da Marco Anzoletti. Milano: Ricordi. Ed. n. E.R. 227.

Corti, Mario (1949). Prefazione alle sonate e partite per violino solo di G. S. Bach. Roma: De Santis.

Faticoni, Cesare (1987). Tre sonate e tre partite per violino solo. Cagliari: Stampa P. Pisano.

Gulli, Franco (2003). Sonate e partite per violino. Revisione di Franco Gulli. Milano: Suvini Zerboni. Ed. n. S12555Z.

Maglioni, Gioacchino (1956). Sonate e Partite per violino solo di Gioacchino Maglioni. Milano: Ricordi. Ed. n. E.R. 2477.

Pinelli, Ettore (1887). Sonate per violin solo. Ed. riv. Da E. Pinelli, per uso del Liceo Musicale della R. Accademia di Santa Cecilia di Roma. Milano: R. Stabilimento musicale Ricordi. N. l. 0000051020.

Polo, Enrico (1933). 6 Sonate e Partite per violino. Revisione fatta sull'edizione della Bach-Gesellschaft. Arcate e segni d'interpretazione a cura di Enrico Polo. Milano: Ricordi. Ed. n. E.R. 1618.

Poltronieri, Alceo (1946). 6 Sonate e partite per violino. Revisione di A. Poltronieri. Milano: Carisch. Ed. n. 20091.

---

[9] Sigiswald Kuijken performed *Sonata* and *Partita n. 1* BWV 1001 and 1002 and the *Partita n. 2* BWV 1004 at the Chiesa di San Rocco in Rome (December 13th, 1983) in the frame of concerts organized by the Società Italiana del Flauto Dolce (SIFD).

Discography

Accardo, Salvatore (1976). Johann Sebastian Bach. Sonatas & Partitas BWV 1001-1006. 3 LPs 33 rpm. Philips. 9500147-149 (1996, 2 CDs, Philips, 459812).

Accardo, Salvatore (2007). Johann Sebastian Bach. Sonata I, II, III – Partite I, II, III per violino solo. 3 CDs. Foné. 90F27/1-3.

De Vito, Gioconda (1947). Ciaccona n. 4 in Re Minore dalla Partita n. 2 per violino solo. 2 LPs 78rpm. La Voce del Padrone. DB 6632-33.

De Vito, Gioconda (1951). Courante dalla Sonata n. 4 in re minore, Sarabanda dalla Sonata n. 4 in re m. 1 LPs 78rpm. La Voce del Padrone. DB 21063.

Gulli, Franco (1973). Sonata n. 2 in Sol minore per violino solo BWV 1001, Sonata per violino e pianoforte "Trillo del Diavolo". LP 33rpm. Angelicum. STA8952 (1979, LP, Ars Nova, VST6178).

Kuijken, Sigiswald (1981). Bach Sonatas (BWV 1001-1006). 1 LP 33 rpm. Deutsche Harmonia Mundi. 77043.

Michelucci, Roberto (1988). Johann Sebastian Bach. Sonata I, II, III – Partite I, II, III. 3 CDs. Foné. 90F27/1-3.

Ughi, Uto (1981). Bach/Ughi. Sonata n. 2, Partita n. 2. LP 33rpm. RCA. RL 31576.

Ughi, Uto (1991). Johann Sebastian Bach. Sonatas & Partitas BWV 1001-1006. 2 CDs. RCA. RD 60971.

Ughi, Uto (2005). J. S. Bach. Sonatas. 2 CDs. Stradivarius. RSTR 005 06.

References

Borghesi, Maria (2019a). *Italian Reception of Johann Sebastian Bach (1950-2000). Words, Sounds, and Ideas.* Dresden: Hochschule für Musik (PhD Dissertation).

Borghesi, Maria (2019b). "Edizioni, registrazioni e generazioni a confronto. Le *Suites* per violoncello solo di Johann Sebastian Bach in Italia". *Per Archi*, 11.

Fabian, Dorottya (2005). "Toward a Performance History of Bach's Sonatas and Partitas for Solo Violin", in L. Vikárius and V. Lampert (eds). *Essay in Honor of László Somfai.* Lamham, MD: Scarecrow Press, pp. 87-108.

Fabian, Dorottya (2015). *A Musicology of Performance. Theory and Method Based on Bach's Solos for Violin.* Cambridge: Open Book Publishers.

Fabian, Dorottya (2017). "Analyzing Difference in Recordings of Bach's Violin Solo with a Lead from Gilles Deleuze". *Music Theory Online.* 23 (4), December 2017, http://mtosmt.org/issues/mto.17.23.4/mto.17.23.4.fabian.html

Lugaresi, Silvana (1985). "Johann Sebastian Bach. Lo conosciamo da trecento anni, proviamo a studiarlo". *Musica Viva,* 9 (3), pp. 49-61.

Chapter 4

Bach in Latin America: good and bad uses of his figure in music education

by Francisco Castillo G.

Universidad Distrital Francisco José de Caldas, Bogotà, Colombia

Music education in Latin America (LA) faces several challenges, and overcoming a Eurocentric history made by biographies of canonical composers is one of them. This paper identifies different uses of Johann Sebastian Bach that music education has made in LA. The conclusions herein presented try to observe this phenomenon and suggest some questions about LA's role in the field of musicological studies. Although this research started in the local context of Bogotá, Colombia, I am trying to extend some of the observations to a broader perspective. The process does not begin by reviewing the set of pedagogical approaches originated in LA; quite contrary, the discussion arises from questions that musicology has been asking in LA for several decades, in which the historical figure of J. S. Bach has had a significant role.

Having been politically and culturally integrated into Europe throughout the seventeenth century, diverse intellectual traditions use the expression 'Latin American Baroque' to refer to music produced in cathedrals and teaching centers from Mexico to Chile. On the other hand, J. S. Bach's figure emerges as the best expression of Baroque music to anyone who seeks to understand the Baroque period. History texts, blog entries, media playlists, and the conventional musicological discourse have turned Bach into the representative musician of the period, to the extent of suggesting that the Baroque era ends in 1750. Imagining Bach as the pinnacle of the Baroque period offers several challenges for the Latin American scene. Although Bach's representativeness can be discussed in the general context of the Baroque, the fact is that Latin American music from the seventeenth and eighteenth centuries owes much more to the Spanish influence than to the Lutheran's.

Establishing Bach as such a model places local composers in a bad position because they do not fulfill expectations when their music is compared with the cantatas composed in Leipzig by the great Johann Sebastian. To some extent, this position reflects the bias in the negative valuation of music that does not meet the standards of technical complexity, reducing it to exotic and primitive manifestations. It should be mentioned that most musicologists move away from these exclusive and arrogant ratings; yet, Bach is very frequently used as an example in LA.

When Jorge Price recounts the details of how the National Music Academy was established in Bogotá,[1] he points out: “Then I gave myself to the task of writing, translating, and printing all the necessary methods and knowledge to achieve a happy success" (1978). Among other books, Stainer's *Theory of Harmony Founded on the Tempered Scale* (1871) stands out. The text contains many examples of Bach's chorales as a model of good harmonic progressions, or as proper uses of chords. It is a fact that the general idea we have of a fugue, counterpoint and tonal harmony in LA, fed by musical education, has been monopolized by the figure of Johann Sebastian Bach (Trotta, 2011). Besides its bias, this approach responds to some pedagogical practicality, and to a wrong line of reasoning as well. There are some theoretical rules for which Bach is a good example, precisely because these rules have been elaborated based on Bach's work.

Performance has not escaped this trend. The Concert Hall at the BLAA[2] in Bogotá is one of the most significant venues in the local scene for performance students. When it came to 50 years of existence in 2015, Cortés (2015) reviewed various data on the musical activity of the hall: the most frequent musician was Bach with 1,220 recurrences. On the other hand, the first round for a recent competition for the position as a violinist of one of the symphony orchestras in Bogotá in 2018, the *Orquesta Filarmónica de Bogotá*, explicitly asked for two contrasting movements of one of Bach's sonatas or partitas. These examples serve as evidence of the special role of Bach's music in the current professional and undergraduate environment.

Inside music classrooms, the situation is not any different. Leaving aside the many uses of Bach among classical musicians, instruments closer to traditional music such as the electric bass, the saxophone, or the *bandola* make constant use of Bach's music. When I asked teachers and students to explain the reasons that led them to play Bach instead of playing their own repertoire, they all answered the same thing: Bach is a technical challenge. Playing a cello suite on electric bass is a way to test the level of technical proficiency. The discussion

---

[1] Currently *Conservatorio de Música de la Facultad de Artes de la Universidad Nacional de Colombia.*

[2] Sala de Conciertos de la Biblioteca Luis Ángel Arango, Bogotá.

here does not concern HIP, rather the use of Bach as an example of difficult music and personal achievement. When I ask students why Bach and not one of Couperin´s suites, it is noted that Bach's presence responds to the reinforcement made by musicological and historical narratives.

If we look closely at relevant aspects in Western music such as harmony, we notice that they are not spontaneous inventions of a brilliant and singular mind. However, historical narratives are prone to simplify these complex processes by identifying "precursory fathers." Perhaps the origin of the myth can be linked to the letter that Beethoven wrote to Hoffmeister: "That you wish to publish the works of Sebastian Bach cheers my heart, which beats warmly to the great artistry of this father of harmony" (in Boyd, 1986). So if Bach is the father, what degree of familiarity do the composers of traditional Latin American music have, especially in cases where only two chords are used? Thus, placing Bach as a father figure reinforces the attitude of cultural superiority that has characterized some musicological discourses.

The case for equal temperament can be read in the same perspective. A book published in Mexico during the 60s titled *What is the history of music?* presented an argument about tuning and temperament that would become recurrent in many conversations according to which Bach invented the modern system of tuning. "We can very well imagine the joy of the ingenious composer who discovered the way to put an F-sharp or a B-flat between the white keys" (Harman, 1958). The point here is not to disentitle Bach as the father and transfer this distinction to Werckmeister. Perhaps as a legacy from the naturalistic approach of musicology in the early twentieth century, we are likely to reference historical events not as part of a complex network of influences, but as organisms that are born, grow, and die.

Another common place in western historiography is to portray musicians as heroes who overcome the obstacles that fate imposes on them. Biographers know that their stories are much more shocking if they highlight the unhappy events of a hero's life, showing their production as a gesture of personal improvement. Perhaps the case of the musician who overcomes obstacles to succeed in music is very attractive within the Latin American context, considering the profound difficulties that our countries are experiencing. Among others, Soler's book (2015) places Bach as a model of personal improvement and psychological strength, even suggesting that "Bach never ceased to fight in the midst of the painful uncertainty of his defeat (...) seemingly inspired by a superior force," and placing Bach "among all the great, victorious combatants of the spiritual realm." (Paumgartner, 1969). Such are examples of the tone that is often used to present figures like Bach as romantic epics of immortal geniuses.

To sum up, among the many uses of Bach within music education in LA, this paper has focused on Bach as a representative of the Baroque period, a model of complexity, the founder of harmony and temperament, and as a personal story of success. How have these visions of Bach impacted the way in which LA thinks about its own music?

Since the colonial project began to introduce cultural values from Europe to the rest of the world, 'the West' began to adopt a cultural place rather than a geographical one. If we recognize that LA is part of the West, the historical narrative of our Western culture seems to establish a quality parameter that includes Bach as its main actor and which places LA far from the canon. Traditional musicology has offered music education a very powerful tool, and that is to think that the canon and the music are the same. LA has adopted this idea supported on figures such as J. S. Bach. In the common story, Bach feeds a vision in which musical works are unique expressions, almost magical, with a defined name, with great and complex features, and with established authorship.

Where does the problem lie? In many cases of Latin American music, asking for the composer's name of a musical work doesn't make any sense. It lacks any sense because words like 'authorship,' 'composition,' and 'work' lack meaning. They are not musical works in a museal sense, nor were they composed by anyone. As they are changing manifestations of a cultural reality, the usual categories are insufficient. In that sense, music education, influenced by the aforementioned uses of Bach, has contributed to hiding the practices, dances, *musicking*, and all non-objective dimensions of music. This situation has led musicology in LA to act in a protectionist way, arguing that local traditions safeguard something vital for the structure of national identity. As posed by Bartók and Kodaly, many researchers understood the relationship between local and European music as a constant struggle to remain pure from colonial influences. This approach has suggested a binary scenario to Latin American music education: either it surrenders to European aesthetics, or it distances itself from it to remain pure.

This dilemma implies a very high risk, as it can hide other sides of the musical phenomenon that are scarcely appreciated by traditional musicological tools. Regarding the preservation of songs, for example, oral tradition is a key element within many local kinds of music. Next to it, there are other practices in which dance, mistakes, or party are key aspects of music. It is a well-known fact that music only occurs inside a cultural context, that these contexts behave in complex ways, and that it is impossible for a culture to remain unpolluted.

To conclude, we should better focus on what we can gain in the future. If teachers and students think about the underlying principles of music education, they will be better equipped to use long-lasting musicological tools as well as to see the relationship between local music and the canonical music outside the winner-loser frame. Becoming aware of Bach's place in our context opens the opportunity to establish a more balanced relationship with European culture in which both are part of the same cultural unity without abandoning their own specificities. The good news is that musicology has also changed, not only to conform to the needs of non-European music, but also to address canonical repertoire from a cultural perspective. My problem is not with Bach as a composer. Bach's music is wonderful in every sense. But being aware of the implications of this Bach-like figure that musicology has created should enable us to think more about non-canonical music, music education, and especially about the ways in which these ideas become part of our musical experience.

Rethinking Bach's place in Latin American music education has not only led us to better understand the ways we think about music. Rather, it has allowed us to find a new Bach. Leaving aside the genius composer and embracing the teacher, Bach fits very well for music in LA: his pedagogical work seems to suggest a 'learning-from-experience' process. Bach may very well remind us that improvisation is not only intended for jazz musicians, and that composition and performance are two sides of the same coin.

References

Boyd, M. (1986). *Bach.* Barcelona: Salvat.

Cortés, J. (2015). "50 años de programación musical de la Sala de Conciertos de la Biblioteca Luis Ángel Arango", in *Si las paredes hablaran: 50 años de música en la Biblioteca Luis Ángel Arango.* Bogotá: Banco de la República.

Harman, C. (1958), *¿Cuál es la historia de la música?.* Mexico: Novaro.

Orquesta Filarmónica de Bogotá, (2018). *Convocatoria Violín No. 001 de 2018.* [online] Available at: https://filarmonicabogota.gov.co/convocatoria-violin-no-001-2018-la-orquesta-filarmonica-bogota (Accessed 17 Jul. 2019).

Paumgartner, B. (1969). *Los Hombres de la Historia: Bach.* Buenos Aires: Centro editor de América Latina.

Price, J. (1978). Datos sobre la Historia de la Música en Colombia. In: H. de Greiff, ed., *Textos sobre música y Folklor,* 1st ed. Bogotá: Instituto Colombiano de Cultura, pp. 258-281.

Soler, J. (2015).*J. S. Bach: una estructura del dolor.* Madrid: Antonio Machado Libros.

Stainer, J. (1871). *A Theory of Harmony Founded on the Tempered Scale, with Questions and Exercises for the Use of Students.* 1st ed. [pdf] London: Rivington. Available at: https://archive.org/details/atheoryharmonyf00staigoog/page/n4 (Accessed 17 Jul. 2019).

Trotta, F. (2011). "Criterios de calidad en la música popular: el caso de la samba brasileña", in J. Sans and R. López Cano (eds)., *Música popular y juicios de valor: una reflexión desde América Latina,* 1st ed. Caracas: Fundación Celarg. pp. 99-133.

Part II

Chapter 5

The futurist movement in Leo Ornstein's early piano solo music[1]

by Andrés Felipe Molano Ruiz

University of Aveiro, Portugal

The aims of this work are:

1. To base an interpretation of Leo Ornstein's early solo piano works on the academic parameters and features of the Futurist movement, displaying their melodic nature.

2. To contribute to a better understanding of the Futurist movement.

Mark A. Radice, in his article "Futurismo: Its Origins, Context, Repertory, and Influence" besides criticising the Futurist movement for its imprecision in writing rhythm, does not mention the influence of the movement on the early piano works of the bad boys[2], composers who studied mostly in the United States of America and especially Ornstein. Emanuele Arciuli tries to relate Futurism to other avant-garde movements, also implying a duality between the academic and anti-academic and contemplating the use of conventional instruments, such as the piano, notation and academic forms, combined with noises, widely studied by the futurist Luigi Russolo.

---

[1] This work is based on a lecture-recital as a PhD student at the University of Aveiro (research unit: INET-MD), during the AEMC conference in Montecassiano (Italy). I am grateful to my main and secondary advisers, Helena Santana and Shao Ling, for their lessons and interest in my research. I would also like to thank the AEMC committee for the opportunity and Severo Ornstein, who gave me permission to quote and record the music of his father Leo Ornstein.

[2] Leo Ornstein, Henry Cowell and George Antheil, among others.

The conception of music by composers related to Futurism or the Futurist movement's art does not apply to many of the parameters considered essential to create artistic works in this period. The predominant approach to artistic thought and creation at music academies and conservatoires around the world determines a very hard path that does not allow a different way to conceive and handle sound and its artistic purpose. However, in Ornstein, eclecticism–also sought by the avant-garde–is evident, since he also wrote conservative music that respects the traditional ways.

Complex rhythm

Italian Futurism intended to innovate in several aspects. Trying to take distance from static and academic artforms, the movement used musical rhythm in unexpected and innovative ways. Futurists proposed to counteract impositions regarding the use of the twelve notes in equal temperament and the use of rhythm in simple subdivisions, features that persisted in the early twentieth century. Francisco Balilla Pratella's "Futurist Music: Technical Manifesto" (1911) criticised the stability and the rhythmic continuity proposed by conservatoires, preferring more complex, unequal rhythms (Pratella 1911, p. 81). In my opinion, this feature is evident in works such as *The Cathedral* (see Figure 5.1).

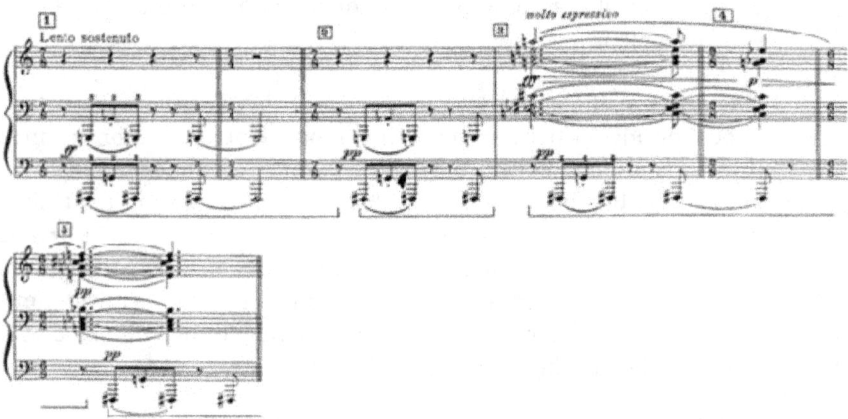

Figure 5.1. The Cathedral.

While it is true that Futurism was rejected in its time, some later vanguard movements highlighted many of the creative principles and ideas that arose from it. After WW II, Futurism sprang in numerous authors and artistic movements, and in contemporary musical and artistic creations. Interest on the absurdness and improvisation of Futurism (Goldberg 1996, pp. 27-28) was present in Ornstein, especially in his renditions of his own music. One of his most interesting qualities as a pianist was his speed, and speed is one of the main characteristics of the Futurist movement as Filippo Tommaso Marinetti wrote in the first futurist manifesto (Marinetti 1909, p. 57). As a young soloist, Ornstein points to the importance of speed in interpretation. According to Michael Broyles and Denise von Glahn, the composer/pianist applied this feature in his performance work, even in music composed outside the Futuristic aesthetic (Broyles and von Glahn 2007).

Futurism tried to highlight the characteristics of the machinery of its time. However, playing at Ornstein's speed while respecting his complex rhythms is a technical and expressive challenge for any pianist. In addition, his piano notation is often uncomfortable, both to read and perform (see Figure 5.2).

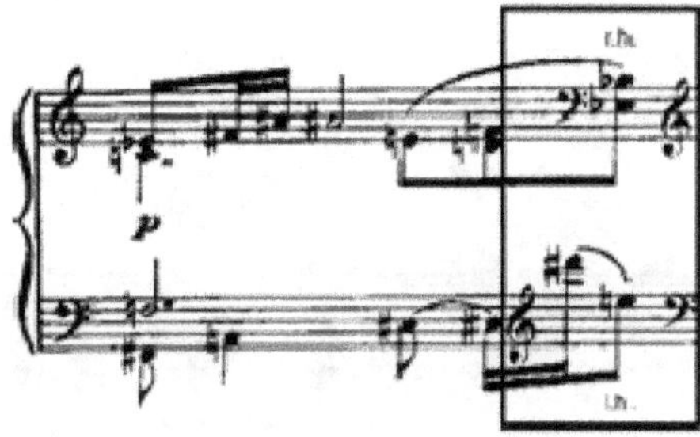

Figure 5.2. Prelude I S057 (own notes in the square).

Noise and melodicism

Regarding rhythm, Ornstein's approach is like Russolo's idea: noise is made up of pitches and rhythms, and within noise, there are distinguishable primary and secondary pitches and rhythms (Russolo 1913, pp. 13-14). This primary/secondary differentiation is possible in Ornstein's repertoire, since it is largely melodic. The innovations proposed by the Futurist movement can be found in his works. For example, his pieces have exotic names as well as far references from Western culture, moreover, pieces with unequal metrics are common in Ornstein's repertoire. In my opinion, this could contribute to different interpretative proposals.

Ornstein's rhythm is also related to the diversity of interpretation present in the Futurist movement and the rhythmic variety that it sought. For example, the simultaneity of dissimilar elements of the futurist theatre (Goldberg 1996, pp. 27-28) is well exemplified in pieces with complex rhythm, melody and noise. The recitals proposed by Ornstein, according to Broyles and von Glahn, exposed a very aggressive piano execution (Broyles and von Glahn 2007). In my opinion, this feature is easy to link with the pretensions of the Futurist movement, this fact is revealing if we consider noise effects in his music, because it can be related to the futuristic noise-tuners[3].

Inventions like the noise-tuners anticipated concrete music. Within this context, it is important to mention a masterpiece of Ornstein's repertoire: *Suicide in an Airplane.* Here, Ornstein evokes one of the most important representations of Futurism. Through tremolos, trills and other effects, confirming his interest in technology and modern life, it is possible to hear one of the symbols of the movement: the airplane (see Figure 5.3).

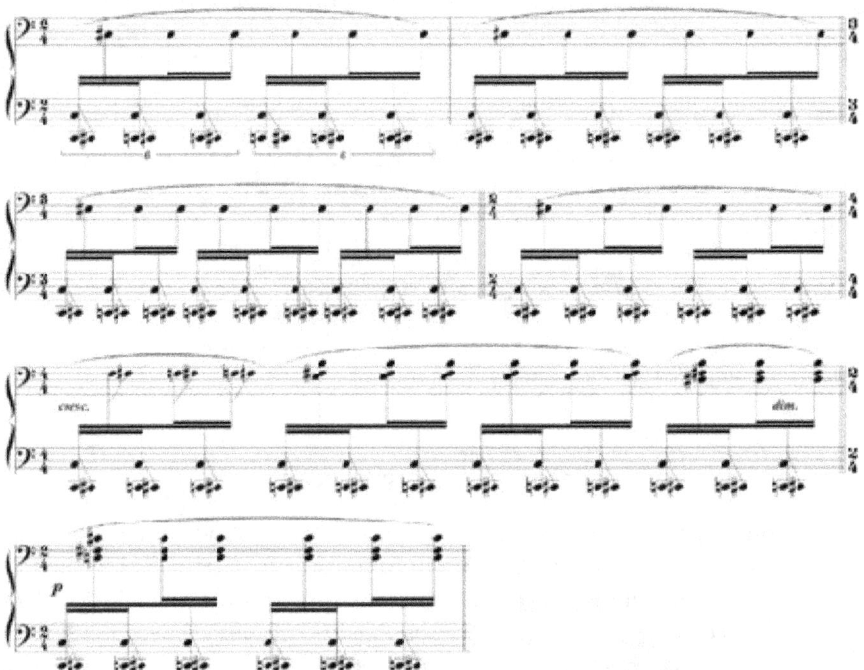

Figure 5.3. Suicide in an Airplane.

3 Instruments invented by Luigi Russolo.

New Musical Resources

Henry Cowell, another of the composers/pianists of my research, mentions a new way to write tuplets in his book *New Musical Resources.* Cowell proposes to change the noteheads, using squares, rectangles, triangles, diamonds, etc. Here, notation is related to a certain subdivision of time or measure (Cowell 2000, p. 56), and it can merge freely when the desired measure or time is completed, to expand the range of the rhythms in use. This notation can be understood both at the rhythmic and harmonic levels. For Cowell, it reveals the immanent property of rhythmic oscillation and its compositional uses.

An analysis of Ornstein's music in Cowell's theory can help to understand the rhythmic, harmonic and formal chaos of some of his scores. Also, in *New Musical Resources,* Cowell states that Eastern musicians use rhythm similarly to his system, and that many Western musicians and singers certainly do not play or sing music as it is written in traditional notation: they always make variations, comparable to the rhythmic subtleties of Cowell's system. Cowell realised that musical notation as used in the West does not show his thinking accurately, nor the musicians' and performers', but only a primary design of the music. In my perspective, Cowell's theory recalls the extent of Russolo's sounds (Radice 1989, pp. 7-10), but now in terms of rhythm.

To obtain satisfactory results, Cowell suggests that to interpret rhythm in his music, it is important to work continuously, albeit succinctly (Cowell 2000, p. 64). This procedure leads to excellence in performance. However, he also states that the music resulting from all these creative and research proposals could be unplayable, given its rhythmic complexity. In order to allow for the viability of his music, Cowell invented the Rhythmicon (Arciuli 2010, p. 87). The ideal of a mechanical instrument for Cowell was partial automation, always maintaining human execution, this way of conceiving mechanical and automated musical performance is certainly distinct from the thinking of Hans Heinz Stuckenschmidt and his discourse about the elimination of the human performer (Patteson 2016, pp. 30-31). It also differs from more conservative stances in academia at time.

The technical and scientific works of Cowell make it possible to consider him as an academic. However, the study of his theoretical works on new ways of composing evidences his distance from the standard academic theories of his time. He was more interested in studying the rhythm and melody of exotic music than the harmonic and contrapuntal tradition of the West. Ornstein echoes this in works like *In the Country* S063 (see Figure 5.4.).

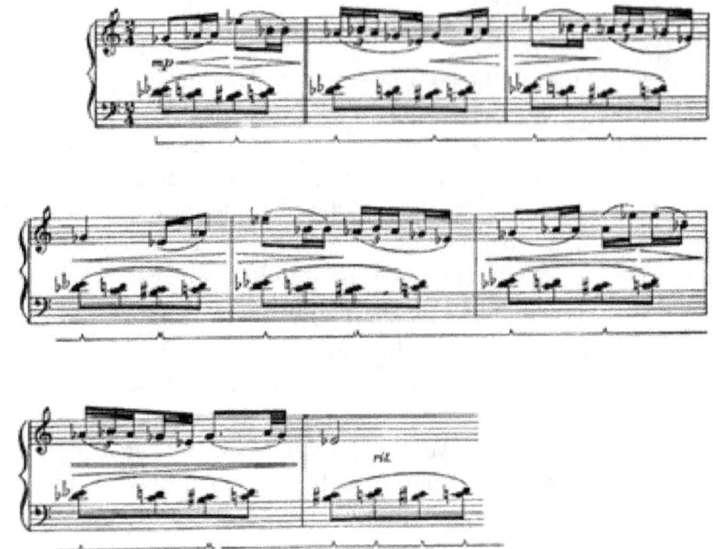

Figure 5.4. In the Country S063.

Conclusion

Maurice Ravel, in works such as *L'enfant et les sortilèges* or his arrangement of Mussorgsky's *Pictures at an Exhibition*, highlights his interest on the Futurist movement. According to Luciano Chessa, Ravel's orchestration shows the sound of the noise-tuners more than any example of recordings of its time (Chessa 2012, p. 150). In my view, this is paradoxical because of the aversion that Russolo had for the symphony orchestra and its audience (Russolo 1913, p. 135). However, the Futurist movement also included proposals that welcomed traditional repertoires, such as the colour/note experiments by Ginani-Corradini. In my opinion, Ornstein's piano compositions display and interpret the sounds of the noise-tuners as well, along with traditional elements such as melodicism, which deserves the special interpretative study pretended in this work. My recording and this text can both serve as responses to the performative and informative aims proposed in the introduction.

While the link between the Italian Futurist movement and fascism is evident, Ornstein's comprehensive eclecticism anticipates the transdisciplinarity advocated by academia today. For me, human interpretation can enrich Ornstein's repertoire with the help of futuristic texts, it is possible to reach an interpretation that does not reject execution by a human. Interpretation purely by machines is still not possible, because the human factor is essential here. For Cowell, up to the publication of *New Musical Resources* (1930), nothing had yet been written that two good pianists could not play. Therefore, as an interpreter, I think it is important not to spare the human effort to perform the works of Futurists and Ornstein, emphasising the rhythmic inequalities, improvisation, freedom of beats, noise, speed and futuristic melody.

References

Arciuli, E. (2010). *Musica per pianoforte negli Stati Uniti.* Turin: EDT.

Broyles, M. and von Glahn, D. (2007). *Leo Ornstein: Modernist Dilemmas, Personal Choices.* Bloomington IN: Indiana University Press.

Chessa, L. (2012). *Russolo, futurist: Noise, Visual Arts, and the Occult.* Los Angeles: University of California Press.

Corra, B. (2002). "Abstract Cinema – Chromatic Music", viewed 5 January 2019, <https://www.unknown.nu/futurism/abstract.html

Cowell, H. (2000). *New Musical Resources.* Cambridge: Cambridge University Press.

Goldberg, R. (1996). *Performance Art.* Barcelona: Ediciones Destino

Ornstein, L. (2006). *Scores.* Poon Hill Press, viewed 9 July 2019, <http://poonhill.com/list_of_works.htm

Patteson, T. (2016). "The Joy of Precision: Mechanical Instruments and the Aesthetics of Automation", in *Instruments for New Music: Sound, Technology, and Modernism.* Oakland: University of California Press, pp. 18-51, viewed 9 July 2019, <http://www.jstor.org/stable/10.1525/j.ctt1ffjn9k.6>

Radice, M. (1989). "Futurismo: Its Origins, Context, Repertory, and Influence", *The Musical Quarterly,* vol. 73, no. 1, pp. 1–17, viewed 9 July 2019, <http://www.jstor.org/stable/741856>

Rainey, L., Poggi, C. & Wittman, L. (2009). *Futurism: An Anthology.* New Haven: Yale University Press.

Chapter 6

Two art song versions of Leopardi's *L'Infinito*

by Alberto Nones

Associazione Europea di Musica e Comunicazione (AEMC), Italy; Conservatory of Music of Gallarate, Italy

Exactly two hundred years ago, one of the most beautiful and beloved Italian poems was written, *L'Infinito* (*The Infinite*) by Leopardi. This paper focuses on two art songs based on it. Giacomo Leopardi (29 June 1798 – 14 June 1837) is the greatest Italian poet of the nineteenth century and one of the most important European figures in literature and philosophy. He was born in Recanati, a few kilometers from Montecassiano,[1] and in *L'Infinito* he portrays the landscape he saw from a garden close to his home, basically the same view one can see from Montecassiano: the countryside with the Potenza river, the fields and isolated farms, the hills, a few villages and towns on top of them, and in the background the faraway chain of the Sibillini mountains. But the poem is not so much about this landscape as it is about a hedgerow, a curtain of greenery that prevents the viewer from reaching the distance, the infinite. This is precisely the engine, the power to ignite imagination. We start to imagine what is beyond when we are not satisfied by what lies visibly before us. This is the core tenet of the poem.

One can give content and form to the aforementioned concept, though, in more than one way. One is negative, pessimistic. And this is the traditional reading of Leopardi's body of poetry and philosophy, a reading that was spread for decades if not centuries. Life is miserable, nature is evil, both deceive us with hopes we are doomed to never achieve. These are for many the defining elements of Leopardi. Lately, however, a new approach to Leopardi's work has

---

[1] Montecassiano is the village where the 2nd AEMC Conference on Music, Communication and Performance was held.

taken the fore (even in the form of a recent movie, *Il giovane favoloso* by Mario Martone). According to this new view, Leopardi was, especially in his early years, a thoughtful genius who also deeply felt the energy of life. His view of nature and the human condition is clearly negative in some later poems or philosophical reflections, but not so much in 1819, when *L'Infinito* was written. "E il naufragar m'è dolce in questo mare" / "and sweet to me is shipwrecking in such a sea", reads the concluding verse of the poem. A shipwreck is there, or we may be doomed to get there, but this is sweet.

In what sense, sweet? And can music lend its sweet voice here? Can music comment on or even embody the positive or negative, optimistic or pessimistic, hopeful or disillusioned reading of any words? Of course, it can; it is what music is destined to do. Music's use in cinema and tv offers perhaps the most obvious evidence: directors and advertisers know very well that music has a powerful effect on our mind and that it gives cinematic material emotional charge (Blacking 1986, Cook 2005). We should, therefore, be able to understand the different interpretations two composers give of the same literary verses they have set to music, through the music itself.

Two art song versions exist of Leopardi's *L'Infinito* that seem—to me—to embody the two different approaches to Leopardi we have sketched out.[2] One is an art song by Pietro Cimara, a composer known today to a niche of connoisseurs. Pietro Cimara was born in 1887 in Rome, where he studied composition with Ottorino Respighi, Stanislao Falchi and Alessandro Bustini (who will also teach Petrassi and Maderna), and died in Milan in 1967. Aside from traces of information to be found in a few sources (Basso 1985, Rich 2003, Nones 2019), he is a figure wrapped in mystery. He began working at the Costanzi theater in Rome first as a substitute and then as a conductor, and ended up at the Metropolitan in New York where he worked for thirty years beginning in 1928. His untiring commitment as a conductor had almost invariably been in roles of preparation and second performances, and, when he suffered a stroke while conducting Verdi's *La forza del destino* in 1958, he at

---

[2] Not many dared creating a musical version of Leopardi's 1819 idyll, in spite of the fact that Leopardi titled "Canti" and "Canzoni" his poems and professed his profound indebtedness to music, and in spite of the fact that most in *L'Infinito* occurs through the sense of hearing and not of sight (Rondoni 2019: 22 and 24) – or maybe precisely because of all of this. Among the few who did dare, one recalls Gaetano Braga, but his version was not included in the comparison because it originates from the 19th century and has a fully different artistic scope; another version exists which dates to 1929, by Amilcare Zanella (and premiered in Recanati by tenor Beniamino Gigli), not included in the comparison because it is a symphonic poem for tenor, choir and orchestra which could have not been performed in its original version at the conference.

once left the podium and went back into the darkness. However, he had also composed songs, one of them based on *L'Infinito* by Leopardi. Cimara even took the liberty of repeating the final verse of what is arguably the most untouchable poem of all Italian literature, and, with the complicity of his editors, slightly changed one word, from "ove" to "onde": signs that it may have been an untouchable poem, but Cimara fully made it his own.

He must have abandoned himself into the abyss, the "confused abyss of innumerable and indefinite sensations" into which music "plunges the listener", to use Leopardi's very wording in a September-24-1821 note in his philosophical diary *Zibaldone di pensieri* (Leopardi 1997: 389-90, my tr). From the first piano chords, Cimara seems to be pointing beyond the hedgerow of the usual frequencies, beyond the curtain of the central area of our emotional keyboard. The four introductory bars of this composition can be seen as Cimara's trait: indefinite or, in a Leopardian sense, vague and hence poetic. The composer takes us on a modulation through six chords, from A minor to C major, ascending in tones and thus creating with the bass line a hexatonic scale. Without it being made overtly explicit in the musical notation, E sharp is enharmonically F, the subdominant of the all-white tonality of C major in which the song is set. At the end of the eighteenth century, poet and theorist Schubart had decreed C major as pure, associating it with a character of "innocence, simplicity, naivety, baby-talk" (DuBois 1983: 433). And Cimara seems to know how to speak with the richness of a child's voice. Let us start by looking at the tempo and agogics. Cimara indicates as a general tempo "Calmo e sereno" / "Calm and serene", which is arguably already an indication of his interpretation of the poem: nothing will be gloomy here; a sense of freedom dominates the scene, never frantic—even though the music is continuous and all-enveloping except for a very brief rest after the piano introduction—and mainly "dolce e tranquillo" / "sweet and quiet". In correspondence with verses where the music could get darker ("e sovrumani silenzi e profondissima quiete" / "and a superhuman silence, and a most profound stillness"), Cimara reinforces "calmo assai" / "very calm". In apparent accordance with the reading that "a lot of things happen" (Rondoni 2019: 20) in a poem which develops through the magnifying power of Leopardi's "pensiero poetante" (Prete 1980), Cimara creates an art song in which musical things happen through structure: he inserts a slightly faster central section, "Poco più mosso", at the point of the poem where the wind comes in, but more generally the whole development triggers a spiral towards the ff and towards the "suon di lei" / "the sound of life, of the present season". After this climax, the tempo returns to the beginning and the song ends, on a sense of reached freedom. Regarding the extension of the voice, A5 (the highest note) is hit four times, returning to the peak of energy through a sustained series of reinforcements; the lowest note is E4, sung just once, in a melody that generally flies high. As for the harmonic structure, the music revolves around two main tonal poles which are both major, C and A. In *L'Infinito,* Cimara's music seems intended to refer to something overall pleasant,[3] "the voluptuousness of the individual disappearing in the universal life", as nineteenth-century literary critic Francesco De Sanctis wrote commenting upon Leopard's poem (De Sanctis 1959: 623, my tr.). A sweet, voluptuous shipwrecking indeed.

The other music version for voice and piano based on Leopardi's poem which I will analyze is by Mario Castelnuovo-Tedesco (1895-1968), who composed an art song on *L'Infinito* in 1931, two years before Cimara. Castelnuovo-Tedesco needs no presentation, as he is a composer widely and rightly celebrated for his magic pen. His *L'Infinito,* fascinating as it is, can in my view be inscribed in a more traditional interpretation of Leopardi's verses—that is, as pessimistic, although it remains to be seen in what sense and how this can be evidenced through music. It is true, and quite a coincidence, that Castelnuovo-Tedesco chooses to set the song in C major just like Cimara, and begins in this tonality immediately, with no introductory modulation. But after four bars he has already switched to C minor, which is the key in which the first verse is sung (with descending chromaticism in the first three notes): "Sempre caro mi fu quest'ermo colle" / "Always dear to me was this solitary hill". The connotation of "dear" is thus put in a different, more melancholic light, which presents the idea of a disposal to renouncing action. The melody is molded onto the verses in

[3] To point out that minor and major do not straightforwardly correspond to sad and happy is the obvious objection, besides the remarks that the emotions triggered by music are far more complex than such a dichotomy, and that everything in music occurs in context, that is, how chords and notes are used and combined. A contamination between the two modes in terms of their impact on our emotions occurs pervasively in classical music and extends to other genres – I am thinking first of all of jazz and in particular the intermingling of minor and major through the play between melody and chords (and the minor and major *effect* that results) in pieces such as Ahmad Jamal's "If I Find the Way" in the 1986 album *Rossiter Road,* just to give one example. But such a truism needs to be counterbalanced by an insistence on the objective difference in harmonic quality between a minor and major third, and by the body of music theory through the centuries on their psychological effect. Ignoring this difference would make a sentence like the following – by one of the most refined pianists and interpreters of the twentieth century – meaningless: "Chopin has a peculiar characteristic. He tends to compose melodies infused with sadness in major, and to coat with some sort of happiness the minor mode" (Cortot 1986: 37, my tr.). Cortot's sentence implies at once the inadequacy (at least in Chopin) of a sad/happy – minor/major correlation, and to the existence (at least in other composers) of such a correlation.

such a sensitive way that it becomes extremely memorable and easy to sing along, more so than in Cimara to my mind, and an oscillation of chords around the basic ones, a chromatic oscillation, up and down by semitones and tones, very aptly recalls the see-through metaphor suggested by the hedgerow. At the same time, the somewhat medieval-sounding parallel fifths and octaves establish a sort of churchly—or unworldly—severity. Let us recall that Castelnuovo-Tedesco had studied with Ildebrando Pizzetti, who invited his student to write a fugue a day to master a Bachian contrapunctum, which arguably allowed Castelnuovo-Tedesco many years later to write his monumental "Les guitares bien tempérées" op. 199 in only three months. Let us return to "L'Infinito" and consider the tempo. Castelnuovo-Tedesco sets it as "Calmo e contemplativo (lentissimo)" / "Calm and contemplative (very slow)", a slower tempo than in Cimara and with a qualification on the "contemplative" that seems to capture Castelnuovo-Tedesco's reading of the poem. The composer's further insistence on "Lentissimo" and "molto lento" reminds the performers not to forget to really keep the tempo slow—a tempo that is poignantly stopped at the rest after the word "silenzi" / "silence". Interestingly, there is a central section in Castelnuovo-Tedesco too, corresponding to the moment in the poem where the wind enters, and it is "Un poco più mosso" and in A major just like in Cimara.[4] A defining difference between the two developments, however, is that Castelnuovo-Tedesco changes harmonies more pervasively throughout, C major reemerging only in the last two bars of the composition, all the rest being a wandering among fairly distant chords. Schubart's baby-talk and naivety of C major are therefore, by necessity, less present in Castelnuovo-Tedesco than in Cimara, or even, one may be tempted to say, they are alluded to but artfully avoided, which is in itself quite profound. Contrasting with the harmonic richness of the piece, there is in Castelnuovo-Tedesco's rendition a certain monastic chastisement as far as the voice is concerned. Indeed, the song seems to be conceived more for a mezzo than for a soprano, which is not by chance: the highest note is G5, a tone below Cimara, and it's not repeatedly reached but sung only once, at the very end upon the return to C major; in the section where the wind comes in, instead, the highest note is one tone below that, F5; the lowest note for the voice is C4, quite low, corresponding to the verse "ove per poco il cor non si spaura" / "to the point that my heart is almost overwhelmed".

---

[4] It is possible that Cimara knew Castelnuovo-Tedesco's work on Leopardi, but I have not found evidence for this. Both composers, for sure, were active in the US, although Castelnuovo-Tedesco moved there – to escape the racial laws of fascist Italy – only in 1939, many years after Cimara and the composition of the song.

One could be tempted to conclude, from this analysis, that the composition by Castelnuovo-Tedesco, solemnly dedicated to another towering figure of the Italian music scene (his master Ildebrando Pizzetti), would emphasize the thoughtfulness of the poem by a (pessimist?) philosopher, whereas Cimara's composition, without dedication and written by a semi-unknown composer, would preserve more lyrically (or more naively?) all the life that palpitates in the poem of a young man. There are elements to this, but all in all, I remain hesitant, especially when going back to performing and listening to the music, aside from reading the score.

For is one version truer to the poem than the other? Not quite. Cimara's art song is true to the way in which Cimara understood and felt the poem just like Castelnuovo-Tedesco's is. The text of Leopardi's poem is reported below (Leopardi 1987), in the original and in my translation, and in the CD attached one can also find a performance of the two songs. Listening to them will allow the readers to decide on their own the extent to which this analysis of the two compositions corresponds to their own perceptions and impressions, and which art song version of Leopardi's *The Infinite* is the truer for them, given their own understanding of the poem and the overall spiritual state of the finite moment in which they will read the verses and listen to the music. Or rather: the finite moment in which they will listen to a performance, and hence to an interpretation, of these art songs.

L'Infinito
by Giacomo Leopardi

Sempre caro mi fu quest'ermo colle,
E questa siepe, che da tanta parte
Dell'ultimo orizzonte il guardo esclude.
Ma sedendo e mirando, interminati
Spazi di là da quella, e sovrumani
Silenzi, e profondissima quiete
Io nel pensier mi fingo; ove per poco
Il cor non si spaura. E come il vento
Odo stormir tra queste piante, io quello
Infinito silenzio a questa voce
Vo comparando: e mi sovvien l'eterno,
E le morte stagioni, e la presente
E viva, e il suon di lei. Così tra questa
Immensità s'annega il pensier mio:
E il naufragar m'è dolce in questo mare.

The Infinite
by Giacomo Leopardi

Always dear to me was this solitary hill,
And this hedgerow, hiding most
Of the furthest horizon.
But when I sit and gaze, I imagine endless
Spaces beyond the hedgerow, and a
Superhuman silence, and a most profound
Stillness, to the point that my heart
Is almost overwhelmed. And as I hear
The wind rustling through these trees, I
Compare that infinite silence to this voice:
And eternity occurs to me,
And all the seasons past, and the present one,
Living and sounding. This way, into this
Immensity, my thought drowns:
And sweet to me is shipwrecking in such a sea.

References

Basso, A., ed. (1985). *Dizionario enciclopedico universale della musica e dei musicisti.* Le biografie vol. II, Torino: UTET.

Blacking, J. (1986). *Com'è musicale l'uomo?* Milano, Ricordi: LIM (*How Musical is Man?* Seattle-London: University of Washington Press, 1973).

Cook, N. (2005). *Musica. Una breve introduzione.* Torino: EDT (*Music. A Very Short Introduction.* New York: OUP, 1998).

Cortot, A. (1986). *Corso d'interpretazione. Raccolto e redatto da Jeanne Thieffry – versione italiana di Alberto Curci (VII ed.).* Milano: Curci.

De Sanctis, F. (1959). *Storia antologica della letteratura italiana,* vol. II, Roma: Armando Curcio Editore (first edition 1870).

DuBois, T.A. (1983). *Christian Friedrich Daniel Schubart's "Ideen zu einer Aesthetik der Tonkunst": An Annotated Translation,* PhD dissertation. University of Southern California.

Leopardi, G. (1987). *Poesie e prose,* vol 1. Milano: Mondadori (Meridiani)

_____. (1997). *Leopardi. Tutte le poesie, tutte le prose e Zibaldone,* vol. *Zibaldone.* Roma: Netwon&Compton.

Nones, A. (2019). "Pietro Cimara, L'Infinito. Or All in a How", in *Pietro Cimara, L'Infinito. Art Songs for Soprano and Piano. Nunzia Santodirocco (soprano) and Alberto Nones (piano).* CD with booklet, Osaka: Da Vinci Classics.

Prete, A. (1980). *Il pensiero poetante.* Milano: Feltrinelli.

Rich, M.M. (2003). *Pietro Cimara (1887-1967): His Life, His Work, and Selected Songs,* PhD dissertation. The University of Texas at Austin.

Rondoni, D. (2019). *E come il vento. L'infinito, lo strano bacio del poeta al mondo.* Roma: Fazi.

Chapter 7

New *Piano Études:* a compositional and interpretive perspective

by Marco Alunno and Andrés Gómez Bravo[1]

Universidad EAFIT, Colombia

Introduction

1.1. The composer (Marco Alunno, from now on MA)

The main concept behind the composition of my piano etudes (Alunno, 2019) derives from a reflection on keys' configurations and fingers' patterns, as they are seen as one of the salient characteristics of piano playing, especially for what concerns the development of instrumental techniques. In addition to abstract ideas of construction, other elements intervene to mold and smooth out the asperities of pre-compositional principles. They will be described in the following sections along with the compositional and interpretive strategies that led to the performance of three of the eight etudes in the collection: *Expressive Fingering, Parallel Thirds* and *Broken Octaves.*

1.2. The interpreter (Andrés Gómez Bravo, from now on AGB)

Since one of the main interests of piano etudes is to explore some technical facet of the piano, I will mostly focus my discussion on this aspect. The three etudes exposed in this article deal with rhythmical complexities, repeated notes, voicing, legato, and textural intricacies that deserve some preliminary comments for all the pianists who want to approach this new repertoire.

[1] Marco Alunno, Universidad EAFIT (Medellín, Colombia), malunno@eafit.edu.co, Andrés Gómez Bravo, Universidad EAFIT (Medellín, Colombia), agomezbr@eafit.edu.co

Expressive Fingering

1.3. Composition (MA)

As far as I know, the initial idea might have come from listening to a Bach fugue and paying attention to the circular harmonic progression of the exposition (tonic – dominant – tonic – dominant – etc.). What I was consciously looking for was a repeating harmonic pattern, and a fugue exposition just happened to offer that. In order to implement a piano technique upon this simple concept, I found it all the more natural to overexpress the contrapuntal writing of a fugue and expect fingers' *legato* to dovetail each voice stream. The overall arch-like, formal shape of the etude is due to the increasing number of voices (from 1 to 7, encompassing the full exposition of the fugue) and a mirror-like decrement (from 7 to 1, a full reversed exposition). This reversal is also reflected in the inversion that the fugue subject undergoes one note at a time throughout the piece (Fig. 7.1).

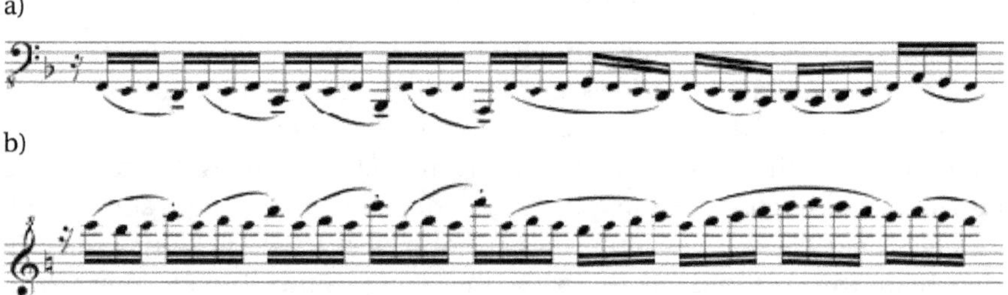

Figure 7.1. Subject of the fugue at the beginning of the piece (a) and its inversion at the end (b).

The subject is original, although it clearly recalls typical Bachian melodic patterns in organ pedaling. The answer is real, but a modification of its tail was necessary to allow a modulation from F to C and back without having to apply an extension, thereby delaying the next entrance of the subject. The idea of the progressive transformation of the subject's melodic profile was certainly inspired by how Sofia Gubaidulina treats Bach's *Musikalisches Opfer*'s theme in her violin concerto *Offertorium* (Gubaidulina, 1990). In this piece, the composer builds a series of variations on Bach's theme and, at each variation, the theme is deconstructed one note at the time and reconstructed back. Thus, as the title suggests, the theme offers itself and comes back to life by mislaying and regaining pieces of its own body. Whereas Gubaidulina took a spiritual reading of the word "offer," in my etude, the fugue subject does not immolate itself, but it is more prosaically morphed into its own inversion.

Such a morphing, though, is not entirely devoid of spiritual accents, for the final, eccentric sprint of the etude is also a leap into the unknown (Fig. 7.2).

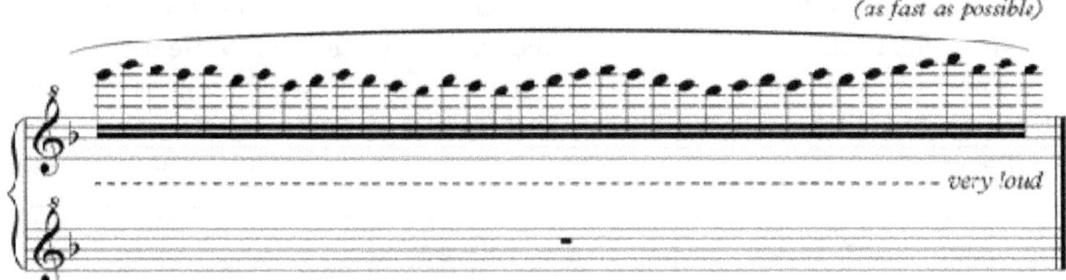

Figure 7.2. Final rush at the end of Expressive Fingering.

Additionally, in order to resist the highly repetitive nature of the harmonic plan of the piece, I was induced to characterize each repetition in a slightly extravagant way. I assigned to each phrase a character indication (e.g., "Imperative", "Confident", "Pompous") that should suggest to the performer a possible interpretation of the music.

1.4. Interpretation (AGB)

Expressive Fingering is more complex to play than it sounds. Even though the tonal language is very familiar to our ear because of the obvious reference to Bach, two features make it difficult to learn. On the one hand, when we think that at the pinnacle of the piece there are seven voices in contrapuntal motion and human beings only have ten fingers, it is quite obvious that some of them have to be doubled or tripled. This creates a problem when reading and playing it, since it is difficult to keep track visually, aurally and manually (referring to the feeling given by depressing the keys) of where each voice is. The second difficulty is that the composer calls for no pedal during the entire etude, which means that the legato passages must be executed using only the fingers. There are passages where, given the disposition of the voices, it is just not possible to keep them pedal-free; thus, some syncopated pedals can rescue the performer. In general, the reasoning behind pedaling in this piece resides in the regular path the etude follows throughout: from the lowest register at the beginning of the piece, where any pedal would muddy the texture, to the highest register of the piano, where some pedal can definitely help in moistening the otherwise very dry sonority of the instrument.

Parallel Thirds

1.5. Composition (MA)

As the subtitle of the etude says ("Vallenato chévere"), the piece was inspired by the typical folk music that originated in the northern Caribbean region of Colombia.[2] A peculiar feature of vallenato music is the sequences of thirds that are played by the accordion, one of the three characteristic instruments in this music genre.[3] Now, what makes it really hard to play parallel intervals on a piano is, of course, the speed the composer asks for (indeed, the character indication for *Parallel Thirds* is "hog-wild").

The speed required to play my etude was not designed to make the pianist's life miserable, it was rather intended to imitate the sound of the *puya,* which is one of the four "airs" or possible rhythmic structures in vallenato music. The *puya* in particular is in 6/8 and is the fastest of the four "airs;" in *Parallel Thirds,* though, the 6/8 meter is frequently reinterpreted as its non-compound version of 3/4. Their alternation in the melodic line reflects the metric ambiguity of *bambuco,* a genre of Colombian folk music from the Andean region. However, whereas in *bambucos* polymetry may be found between the melody (in 6/8) and its accompaniment (in 3/4), in *Parallel Thirds* this principle is extended to the combination of odd meters (such as 6/8 and 3/4) in the melodic line and even meter (4/4) in the harmonic progression (Fig. 7.3).

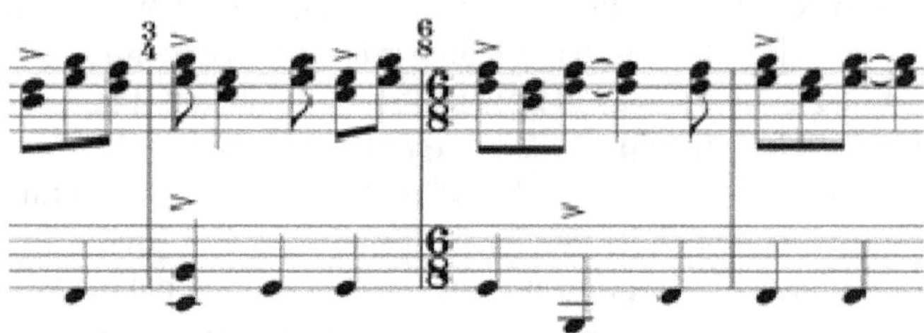

Figure 7.3. Polymetry and heterometry in Parallel Thirds, mm. 30-31.

In Fig. 7.3 one can also observe that, as the harmonic progression reflects the typical simple scheme (I-V-I) of much of folk music, the obvious result of the difference of durations between melodic and harmonic layers yields recurring

[2] The word "chévere" is a Colombian slang expression that means "cool."

[3] The other two are the *caja vallenata* (a small drum) and the *guacharaca* (a scratch-sounding percussive instrument similar to the güiro).

polytonality, namely when dominant harmony is overlapped to the tonic chord implied in the melody. The disorientation generated by polytonality is quickly transformed into clusters, first in the lowest four piano keys only, and eventually in both hands all over the piano keyboard (Fig. 7.4):

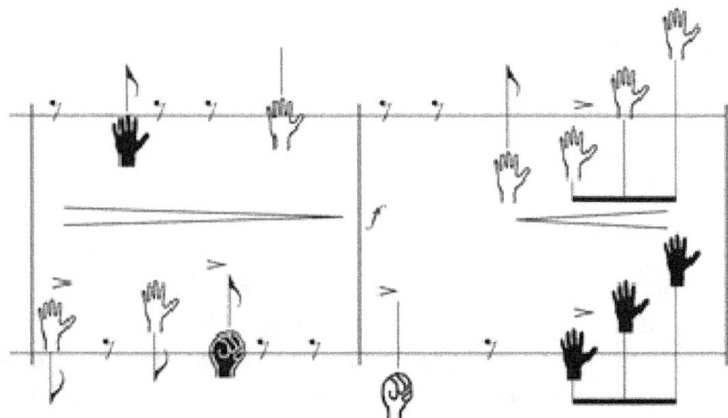

Figure 7.4. Graphic notation for different kinds of clusters, mm. 74-75.

1.6. Interpretation (AGB)

As required by the composer, the speed marked in this etude is almost unattainable. The accordion, whose agility inspired this piece, can play three notes by depressing just one key, which sets the speed limit for that instrument extremely high. On the other hand, the piano and the pianist have two limitations: the mechanics of the instrument, which only allow for repeating the same key at a certain speed, and the lateral movements that are required to play the etude, which also impose some physical limitations.

The indication by the composer is to play non-legato, which makes it especially beneficial when there are two or three notes to be played at the same time by the same hand.

In the last section, where the melodic patterns move by triads, I do not exclusively use the same fingering for every chord. In fact, the leaps make it almost impossible to do so. Rather, I use a combination of 1-2-3, 1-2-4 and 2-3-5 fingering to bridge the leaps, always aiming for the fastest way possible to overcome the passage, thereby resembling the pace of the *puya* (Fig. 7.5).

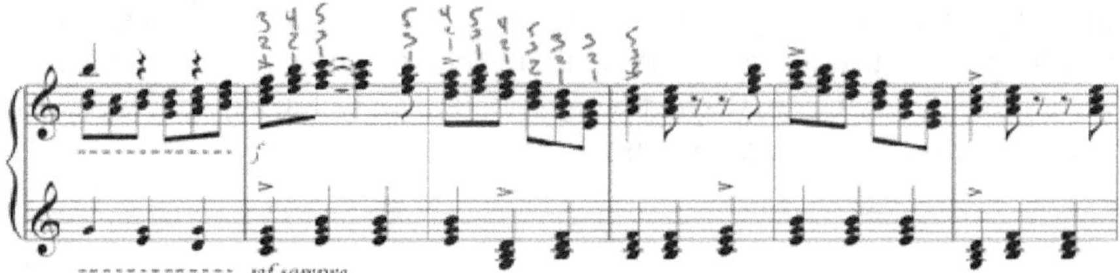

Figure 7.5. Recapitulation with parallel triads and manuscript fingerings, mm. 96-101.

Broken Octaves

1.7. Composition (MA)

This is not a homage to Kōji Kondō, the iconic composer of video game music for the first Nintendo consoles back in the 1980s. This is not a homage simply because in my youth I never played with a Nintendo, thus my acquaintance with that music world is relatively superficial. It is just that while thinking of the broken octaves technique in the piano, I could not prevent myself from recalling one of the many well-known themes Kondō composed in 1985 for the video game *Super Mario Bros.* (hence the ironic subtitle "D'aprés Super Mario Bros."), namely the *Underground Theme* (Fig. 7.6).

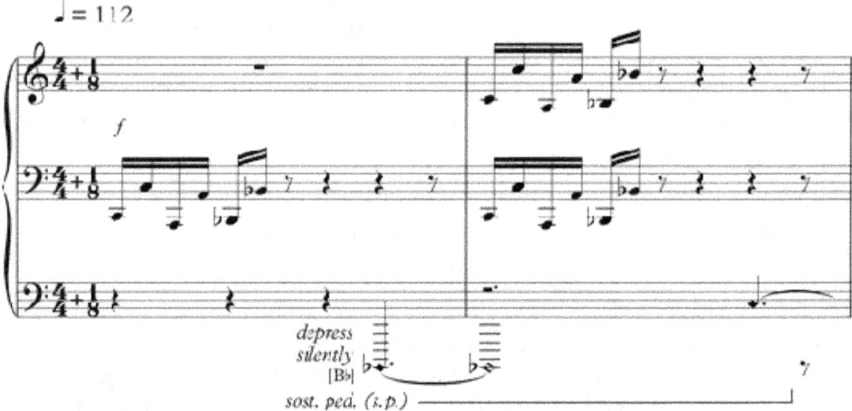

Figure 7.6. Transcription of the Underground Theme in Broken Octaves, mm. 1-2.

If one expects to listen to only tonal music in video games, he/she might be surprised at the chromatism of the *Underground Theme.* In fact, not only the melodic profile of the theme's head reminds of set classes of Webernian flavor, but the whole theme is highly chromatic. Thus is my etude, while it develops through transformations and imitations of the theme's head, the only portion of the *Underground Theme* used in the piece. Of that theme, the etude also inherits a clear robotic pace that is willfully called for in the last section. Finally, observe also how peculiarly the piano sonority is treated with respect to the sound world of *Super Mario Bros.*: whereas the latter was constrained to produce only so-called 8-bit (or chip) music, the former adds to it the resonance that that technology could not provide. The dry, assertive incipit of the *Underground Theme*, enhanced by the sharp decay of the 8-bit sounds is counteracted by the ghostly contrail left by the sostenuto pedal and the muted keys in *Broken Octaves* (Fig. 6 and 7).

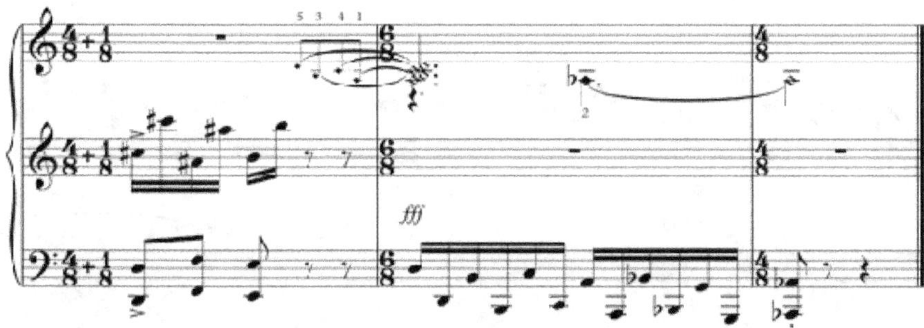

Figure 7.7. Finale of Broken Octaves with resonance effect, mm. 92-94.

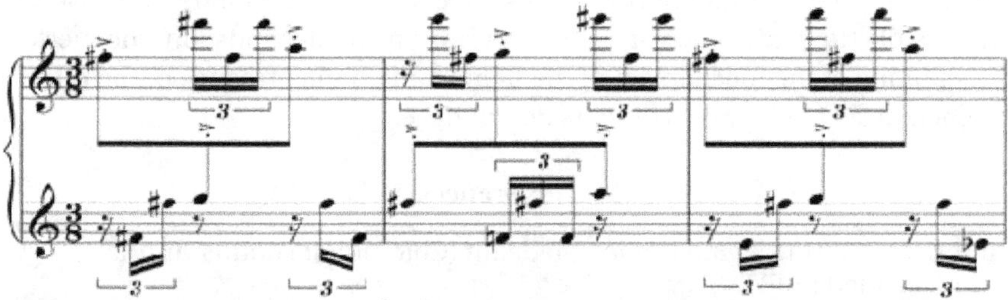

Figure 7.8. Intertwined articulation between hands in Broken Octaves, mm. 27-29.

1.8. Interpretation (AGB)

This etude provides several interesting difficulties. First, we have the obvious ones derived from playing an octave etude, which include lateral movements and the coordination of the two hands. Second, we have the broken octaves, which in this piece move in both directions (up-down and down-up) and includes several triplets as a contrast to duplets. The third problem is the accentuation, particularly in the section that starts in measure 26 and deals with an F#-G-A melodic profile intertwined with triplet movements that expands beyond an octave interval (Fig. 7.8).

Finally, and perhaps most interestingly, there is the fact that the composer uses the harmonic resonance of the piano as a fundamental tool of composition. This is seen in the use of the middle pedal while silently depressing the keys. In my opinion, this etude is a better teaching piece for this specific skill than any other in the repertoire I know, except possibly for Lachenmann's *Serynade* (Lachenmann, 2002). With regard to this, the most difficult place is probably from measure 50, where a sequence of notes that have to be played silently in the left hand comes while the right hand goes up in broken octaves (Fig. 7.9).

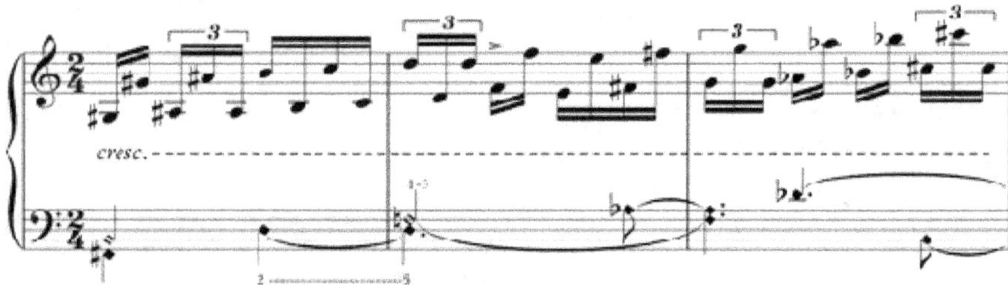

Figure 7.9. Sequence of silent keys in Broken Octaves, mm. 51-53.

It is important to mention that this aspect makes the etude very risky or impossible to play, since a proper performance depends on the perfect functioning of the mechanism of the piano and on the presence of the middle pedal that some older instruments do not have.

References

Alunno, M. (2019). *Piano Études.* Medellín (Colombia): Fondo Editorial Universidad EAFIT.

Gubaidulina, S. (1990). *Offertorium.* Moscow: Sovestky Kompozitor Publishers.

Lachenmann, H. (2002). *Serynade.* Wiesbaden, Germany: Breitkopf & Härtel.

Authors and performers

Marco Alunno is an Italian composer. In his country, he earned a diploma both in piano and composition from the musical institute of his native town, Livorno, and a university degree in Italian Literature (specialization in History and Aesthetic of Cinema) from the University of Florence. Afterwards, he completed his Ph.D. in Composition at the Eastman School of Music (Rochester, NY) where he served as an instructor in composition and Italian cinema. At present, he is a professor of Composition and Theory at the Universidad EAFIT (Medellín, Colombia) where he works also as a researcher in both film music and new technologies. (www.marcoalunno.com)

Chiara Bertoglio is a concert pianist, musicologist and theologian. Her degrees include the Conservatory diploma in Piano (1999), a Master's at the Accademia di S. Cecilia (2003), musicological degrees at the Universities of Venice and Rome, a PhD in Music Performance Practice (Birmingham, 2012) and Master's degrees in Theology (Rome and Nottingham). She is the author of several books in Italian and English, among which the award-winning *Reforming Music. Music and the Religious Reformations of the Sixteenth Century* (De Gruyter, 2017). She performs worldwide as a soloist, and teaches at Italian Conservatories (piano and history of music) as well as in theological universities. She is also a member of the organizing committee of BackTOBach, an international festival in Piedmont.

Maria Borghesi is a PhD candidate in Musicology at the Hochschule für Musik – Dresden: her defense will take place at the end of 2019, and her thesis is entitled "Italian Reception of J. S. Bach (1950-2000): Words, Sounds, and Ideas". In 2018 she obtained a six-months grant at the Deutsches Historisches Institut in Rome; presently she has a contract for the ERC-Project 'Performart' at the École Française de Rome. She collaborates with the Italian Musicological Society and the Bach Network. In July 2018, she led the secretarial team at the "18th Biennial International Conference on Baroque Music" in Cremona.

Francisco Castillo works in the musicology department of the FJdC District University - ASAB in Bogotá. He has been the academic editor of several books on historiography, analysis and music education, and has published articles on musical perception and medieval notation. In addition to teaching music history, his research focuses on the historiography of western music and music education. He is also a performer of early music with the harpsichord and the baroque traverso flute.

Mario Ciferri graduated in Piano, Organ, Conducting, Harpsichord and Sacred Music at the Conservatories of Bologna, Roma and Pesaro. A Rossini Foundation Scholarship recipient in 1993, he also graduated in Conducting from the Music Academy of Pescara, where he studied with Donato Renzetti. As a conductor, he won in 2014 the First Prize at "A. Guanti" International Choral Competition of Matera. He performs regularly as an organist at the most renowned organ festivals in Europe, Russia, Canada and the USA. Among his recordings, the world premiere of the complete works by Luigi Vecchiotti (Bottega Discantica, 2004). He teaches Organ, Gregorian Chant and Harpsichord at the Conservatory of Fermo.

Andrés Gómez Bravo is a Colombian pianist leading a wide career as a soloist, collaborative pianist and teacher. He has performed in festivals and conferences around the world including presentations in Argentina, Finland, Sweden, Italy and Brazil, as well as recitals in Canada, the United States, Australia and New Zealand. As a soloist, he has performed with several Colombian orchestras; as a recording artist, he has participated in 7 CDs. Dr. Gómez has degrees from EAFIT (BM), Eastern Michigan University (MA) and the Eastman School of Music (DMA). He is currently head of the piano department at EAFIT. (www.andresgomezbravo.com)

Gianluca Luisi graduated in Piano with distinction from the Conservatory of Pesaro, where he studied with Franco Scala, and continued his studies with Aldo Ciccolini, besides at the Imola Piano Academy "Incontri col Maestro". A winner of numerous competitions, he received the first prize at the 4th International J. S. Bach competition in Saarbrucken - Würzburg in 2001. Luisi has performed in the most prestigious venues around the world, with a repertoire that ranges from Bach to the twentieth century. His 26 recordings include Bach's Partitas, Suites, and a complete Well-Tempered Clavier that Fanfare and American Record Guide described as an absolute reference, at the level of Edwin Fischer's. He is a Bösendorfer artist and Naxos recording artist. (www.gianlucaluisi.com)

Michael Maul studied Musicology at the University of Leipzig. In 2006 he completed an award-winning dissertation on "Baroque Opera in Leipzig (1693–1720)" at the University of Freiburg and in 2013 completed his prize-winning habilitation thesis "Dero berümbter Chor–Die Leipziger Thomasschule und ihre

Kantoren 1212–1804" (English translation published by Boydell&Brewer in 2018). He is a researcher at the Bach-Archiv in Leipzig, where he also serves as artistic director of the Leipzig Bachfest. Dr. Maul is internationally renowned for several Bach discoveries during the last decade. He is a lecturer in musicology at the Universities of Leipzig and Halle and produces on a regular basis a radio show on J. S. Bach for Deutschlandfunk Kultur.

Alberto Nones graduated with distinction in Piano at the Conservatory of Trento and in Philosophy at the University of Bologna, and further earned an MSc from the London School of Economics and a PhD from the University of Trento. He is the author of four monographs—on Verdi, Zandonai, and The Doors—and many articles. His recordings include *Pietro Cimara L'Infinito, Art songs for soprano and piano* (2019), *Johannes Brahms, The Sonatas for piano and violin* (2017, with Franco Mezzena), and a highly acclaimed *Fryderyk Chopin, The Complete Mazurkas* (2CDs, 2016). The founder and president of AEMC, Dr. Nones also works as a broadcaster of radio programs for the Trento branch of RAI and is the artistic director of various festivals in Italy. He teaches History and Aesthetics of Music at the "G. Puccini" Conservatory of Gallarate. (www.albertonones.com)

Andrés Ruiz, a Colombian pianist, was accepted as a doctoral student in performance at the University of Aveiro (Portugal) with his research project "The futuristic thought in the piano solo repertoire of Leo Ornstein, Henry Cowell and George Antheil". His work was presented at the London International Piano Symposium 2018 (RAM), the Congrès Doctoral International de Musique et Musicologie 2018 (Sorbonne), JIAM 2019 (Museu Cerdà), Diálogos con Egresados UN (Universidad Nacional de Colombia), ENIM 2018 (ESMAE), Hands on Piano 2018 (DECA), Escola de Outono 2018 (DECA), Seminarios Diego Ghymers (Musikeon), etc.

Nunzia Santodirocco graduated in Singing and Piano. Her career led her to sing *Aida* at the Arena of Verona, the Teatro Verdi of Salerino and the Daegu Opera Festival in Korea; *Tosca* at the Cairo Opera House and the Politeama in Lecce; *Madama Butterfly* at the Seoul Arts Center and in Kyoto; *Un ballo in maschera* at the Cervantes Theater in Malaga and at the Politeama of Lecce. She has performed at the Tokyo Opera City Concert Hall, and the Italian Ministry of Foreign Affairs has invited her as representative of *bel canto* throughout the world. Her recordings include *Madama Butterfly* (Ricordi), *Lo sposo burlato* (Bongiovanni), *Giuseppe riconosciuto* by Anfossi (Fonè) and the Complete Oratorios by Carissimi (Brilliant Classics).

Scientific committee

Dr. Ricciarda Belgiojoso (Polytechnic University of Milan, PianoCityMilano)

Professor Monika Fink (University of Innsbruck)

Dr. Michael Maul (Bach-Archiv Leipzig)

Dr. Alberto Nones (AEMC)

Dr. Hamish Robb (Victoria University of Wellington)

AEMC 2019 performances

1.	J. S. Bach (1685-1750), *In dulci jubilo* BWV 751
Mario Ciferri, organ	
2.	M. Alunno (1972-), *Expressive Fingering* (Homage á J. S. Bach)
3.	- *Parallel thirds* (Vallenato chévere)
4.	- *Broken Octaves* (d'après Super Mario Bros)
Andrés Gómez Bravo, piano	
5.	M. Castelnuovo-Tedesco (1895-1968), *L'Infinito* (Leopardi)
6.	P. Cimara (1887-1967), *L'Infinito* (Leopardi)
Nunzia Santodirocco, soprano **Alberto Nones**, piano	
7.	L. Ornstein (1895-2002), *The Cathedral* S073
8.	- *Prelude* n. 1 S057
9.	- *Suicide in an Airplane* S006
10.	- *In the Country* S063: The Gypsy Lament
11.	- *In the Country* S063: The Old Dungeon
12.	- *In the Country* S063: The Cathedral Bells and the Choir
Andrés Ruiz, piano	
	J. S. Bach (1685-1750), *French Suite n.2 in* *C minor, BWV 813*
13.	- Allemande
	- Courante
	- Sarabande
	- Air
	- Menuet – Trio
	- Gigue
Gianluca Luisi, piano	

Live recordings taken in Montecassiano, Italy, on 30 June 2019 at the Church Collegiata (track 1, Callido organ), on 29 June 2019 at the AEMC headquarters in Palazzo Ferri (tracks 2-4), on 29 June 2019 at the Church of San Marco (tracks 13-18) and on 30 June 2019 at the Church of San Marco (tracks 5-12).

Pianos (all from the Nones Collection): track 13-18 C.Bechstein 200cm s.n.13468; track 5-12 August Förster 275cm s.n.529301; track 2-4 Steinway & Sons model B s.n.100369.

Index

H

I

J

K

L

M

O

P

R

S

www.ingramcontent.com/pod-product-compliance
Lightning Source LLC
LaVergne TN
LVHW020655100826
845148LV00012B/2503
* 9 7 8 1 6 2 2 7 3 9 1 5 8 *